PPP and L2TP

ISBN 0-13-022462-6

Prentice Hall Series In
Advanced Communications Technologies

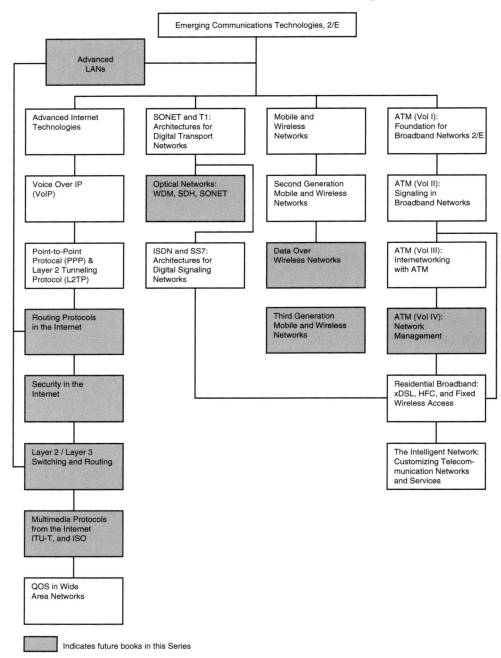

Emerging Communications Technologies, 2/E

Advanced LANs

Advanced Internet Technologies

SONET and T1: Architectures for Digital Transport Networks

Mobile and Wireless Networks

ATM (Vol I): Foundation for Broadband Networks 2/E

Voice Over IP (VoIP)

Optical Networks: WDM, SDH, SONET

Second Generation Mobile and Wireless Networks

ATM (Vol II): Signaling in Broadband Networks

Point-to-Point Protocal (PPP) & Layer 2 Tunneling Protocol (L2TP)

ISDN and SS7: Architectures for Digital Signaling Networks

Data Over Wireless Networks

ATM (Vol III): Internetworking with ATM

Routing Protocols in the Internet

Third Generation Mobile and Wireless Networks

ATM (Vol IV): Network Management

Security in the Internet

Residential Broadband: xDSL, HFC, and Fixed Wireless Access

Layer 2 / Layer 3 Switching and Routing

The Intelligent Network: Customizing Telecommunication Networks and Services

Multimedia Protocols from the Internet ITU-T, and ISO

QOS in Wide Area Networks

Indicates future books in this Series

PPP and L2TP: Remote Access Communications

UYLESS BLACK

Prentice Hall PTR
Upper Saddle River, New Jersey 07458
www.phptr.com

Library of Congress Cataloging-in-Publication Data

Black, Uyless D.
    PPP and L2TP : remote access communications / Uyless Black
      p. cm.
    Includes bibliographical references and index.
    ISBN 0–13–022462–6
    1. PPP (Computer network protocol) 2. L2TP (Computer network protocol) I. Title.

TK5105.582 .B53   1999
004.6′2—dc21   99–047025
                                                                    CIP

Acquisitions editor: *Mary Franz*
Editorial assistant: *Noreen Regina*
Cover designer: *Talar Agasyan*
Cover design director: *Jerry Votta*
Manufacturing manager: *Maura Goldstaub*
Marketing manager: *Lisa Konzelmann*
Project coordinator: *Anne Trowbridge*
Compositor/Production services: *Pine Tree Composition, Inc.*

 © 2000 by Uyless Black
Published by Prentice Hall PTR
Prentice-Hall, Inc.
Upper Saddle River, New Jersey 07458

Prentice Hall books are widely used by corporations and government agencies for training, marketing, and resale.

The publisher offers discounts on this book when ordered in bulk quantities. For more information contact:

Corporate Sales Department
Phone: 800–382–3419
Fax: 201–236–7141
E-mail: corpsales@prenhall.com

Or write:

Prentice Hall PTR
Corp. Sales Dept.
One Lake Street
Upper Saddle River, New Jersey 07458

Printed in the United States of America
10 9 8 7 6 5 4 3 2 1

ISBN: 0–13–022462–6

Prentice-Hall International (UK) Limited, *London*
Prentice-Hall of Australia Pty. Limited, *Sydney*
Prentice-Hall Canada Inc., *Toronto*
Prentice-Hall Hispanoamericana, S.A., *Mexico*
Prentice-Hall of India Private Limited, *New Delhi*
Prentice-Hall of Japan, Inc., *Tokyo*
Pearson Education Asia Pte. Ltd, *Asia*
Editora Prentice-Hall do Brasil, Ltda., *Rio de Janeiro*

*This book is dedicated to
Rose Black*

What image comes to your mind when you read or hear the term "tunnel"? I returned from Europe recently, so my image is the "chunnel" under the English Channel between England and France. In the winter, my image is the tunnel I pass through to get from Denver to Vail to reach the ski slopes.

For the creature for this book in the series, I have chosen the prairie dog. The reason? It is a tunneling creature, and the subject of this book deals with tunnels . . . well, not earth tunnels, but protocol tunnels.

This book deals with the encapsulation of IP traffic onto PPP frames for the transport from one computer to another. In today's jargon, this encapsulation operation is called a tunnel. It is so-named because IP is transported through the PPP tunnel, and while in this "tunnel," IP is not visible to other protocols.

I had originally chosen a mole for this book's cover. I chose this animal against the advice of several people, who said the mole was so unattractive that its appearance would discourage potential buyers of this book. As you can see, the mole was not chosen, and I will explain why. This tiny mammal (about 6 oz.) is a burrowing wonder. It is capable of digging a tunnel at a rate of 18 feet per hour, considerably better than some mechanized burrowing machines. Its tunnels are often berated due to the perception that the mole's tunnels damage plants and trees that are rooted above the tunnel. While this view is somewhat true, the tunnel is also an aerator, often serving useful purposes. And the damage to the flora often comes from other creatures that use the mole's tunnel. For example, mice are often the culprits that eat the roots exposed by the mole's tunnels. The mole does not dig the tunnel to eat the roots. It digs in search of worms, grubs, and small insects—but not your rose bush. On the other hand, the prairie dog is considered a harmless creature.

The analogy I had intended for this write-up was to liken the mole to the PPP tunneling protocol. It creates the tunnel that other creatures may also use. IP is like the mouse—it uses the mole's tunnel to move from one point to another.

Well, the mole analogy did not fare so well when the idea was analyzed by marketing people. In so many words, the mole was too ugly; it would not stimulate a potential reader to open the book if the book were laying on a book shelf in a book store.

It was a revelation to me. I had thought people actually bought books based on their titles and contents. They still do, but an attractive cover entices a person to pick up the book, and browse through it. I had never given it any thought, but studies have confirmed this fact.

Can you imagine my surprise at the discovery of my marketing skills? I had created these creature analogies much for fun, never realizing I was a retailing whiz.

I must admit that I succumbed to my own prejudices when I saw the pictures of the mole and the prairie dog that my publisher gave me, and the mole picture was as flattering a picture of a mole as one would ever see. I think the artist even air-brushed it. Faced with these two choices, you see the results of my decision on the cover of this book.

Why does the picture of the mole harbor unpleasant thoughts to some people? For that matter, what makes one creature attractive, and another repulsive? Why is sushi a delight to one and repugnant to another? Why are some species considered attractive, and others homely? We must leave the questions to the experts in these matters.

But one thing I do know, the vast majority of people, if they had a choice, would rather have a picture of a prairie dog hanging in their homes than a picture of a mole. I know, because I conducted a survey. Therefore, case closed. The prairie dog it is.

Nonetheless, the mole is still on the cover, but you can't see it, because it is inside the tunnel. And I'm on my way to Madison Avenue.

Contents

CHAPTER 3   The Principal PPP Entities: LCP   29

Preface

This book is one in a series of books called, "Emerging Communications Technologies." As the name of the book implies, the focus is on the Point-to-Point Protocol, and the Layer 2 Tunneling Protocol (L2TP).

The subject matter of this book is vast and my approach is to provide a system view of the topic. In consonance with the intent of this series, this general survey also has considerable detail, but not to the level of detail needed to design a system. For that, I leave you to your project team and the various specifications that establish the standards.

This book is considered to be at an intermediate-to-advanced level. As such, it assumes the reader has a background in data communications and the internet protocol suite. Notwithstanding, for the new reader, I have provided several tutorials and guide you to them in the appropriate parts of the book.

I hope you find this book a valuable addition to your library.

CREDITS

I have relied on several Internet Request for Comments (RFCs) and Internet Drafts in certain chapters in this book. In some cases, I have summarized the RFCs with a short tutorial, and in other cases, I have extracted key points from the documents. I have so noted these instances in the appropriate part of the book.

Keep in mind that the Internet Drafts are works in progress, and should be viewed as such. You should not use the drafts with the expectation that they will not change. Notwithstanding, if used as general tutorials, the Drafts discussed in this book are "final enough" to warrant their explanations.

For all the internet standards and draft standards the following applies:

PPP and L2TP

1

Introduction

This chapter introduces the Point-to-Point Protocol (PPP). It explains why PPP was developed by the Internet standards groups, and why it is widely used.

The chapter also explains the concepts of data link protocols and shows how PPP fits into the data link protocol picture. The Network Access Server (NAS) is described in this chapter as well.

WHY PPP WAS DEVELOPED

PPP was implemented to solve a problem that evolved in the industry during the last decade. With the rapid growth of data networks, several vendors and standards organizations developed a number of network-layer protocols (layer 3 or L_3protocols). The Internet Protocol (IP) is the most widely used of these protocols.

As happens when different protocols are developed simultaneously, machines (such as routers) typically must run more than one network-layer protocol. While IP is a given on most machines, routers also support network-layer protocols developed by companies such as Xerox, 3Com, Novell, etc. Machines communicating with each other needed to know which network layer protocols were available to support a user's application.

Moreover, in some situations, it was desirable to be able to negotiate options to be used during a session between two computers. For example, compressing certain parts of the transmitted traffic can yield better throughput on a link. As another example, an Internet Service Provider (ISP) may wish to assign an IP address to its customer. Until PPP was developed, these operations were performed with proprietary protocols, or worse, were not performed (leading to wasted bandwidth in the compression operation and wasted IP address space in the address assignment operation), thus complicating the interworking of different vendors' products.

In addition, until the advent of PPP, the industry did not have a standard means to define a point-to-point encapsulation protocol. Encapsulation means that one protocol carries or encapsulates another protocol's traffic (say, a network layer's traffic) in an information (I) field. The encapsulating protocol uses another field in its header to identify which network layer traffic resides in the I field. Thus, a machine (for example, a router) can examine the encapsulation header in an incoming packet and determine how to process the packet. For example, the packet may be for an IBM L_3 protocol, or it may be for an AppleTalk protocol.

The PPP standard solves these two problems. It provides standardized methods for negotiating a wide variety of operations and options, and it provides encapsulation features.

Moreover, until PPP was developed, the industry relied on older, less-efficient protocols, such as the Serial Link Internet Protocol (SLIP). This protocol was developed several years ago and has been replaced (with some exceptions) by PPP.

WHAT PPP DOES

PPP is used to encapsulate network-layer datagrams over one serial communications link. The protocol allows two machines on a point-to-point communications link to negotiate the particular types of network-layer protocols (such as IP) that are to be used during a session. It also allows the two machines to negotiate other types of operations, such as the use of compression and authentication procedures. After this negotiation occurs, PPP is used to carry the network-layer protocol data units (PDUs) in the information (I) field of the PPP packet.

Typically, the two machines involved in this process are the user node (a workstation, a PC, a router, etc.) and the machine at the service provider (a server node), which could be a router. The server node, whatever the machine may be, is often called a Network Access Server (NAS).

APPLICATIONS OF PPP

PPP is employed in many systems and applications. We will use Figure 1–1 to show some typical scenarios. For residential users and small businesses, a common approach is to dial-in to a data service (say, the Internet) through analog facilities and the Public Switched Telephone Network (PSTN). With this arrangement, PPP is used in conjunction with analog modems to connect to the PSTN and an ISP. Typically, the ISP maintains a modem pool, and a modem is assigned to the connection during the dial-in handshake. The link between the PSTN and the ISP is usually not analog, and is depicted in Figure 1–1 as an ISDN Primary Rate Interface (PRI), which is a digital link.

Some residences and many businesses use an ISDN Basic Rate Interface (BRI) link, typically operating at 64 kbit/s or 128 kbit/s. With this arrangement a terminal adapter (TA) interworks the user's analog interface with the service provider's digital equipment. PPP runs in conjunction with ISDN to support the users' session with the Internet.

On the right side of Figure 1–1 is another common application in which a mobile user dials-in to the Internet. PPP is also used here to set up a connection and negotiate parameters for the connection. PPP operates over a variety of air interfaces. This example shows three: (a) Code

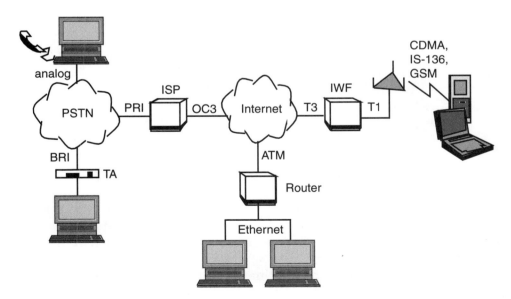

Figure 1–1 Typical system in which PPP operates

Division Multiple Access (CDMA), (b) IS-136, and (c) Global Systems for Mobile Communications (GSM). The Interworking Function (IWF) acts as a gateway between the fixed and mobile networks. It may perform PPP functions with the mobile node, or it may pass the PPP traffic back and forth between an ISP and the mobile node.

At the bottom of Figure 1–1 is yet another configuration. Here, an enterprise connects to the Internet through the enterprise router. The user workstations connect to the router via an Ethernet LAN. With this configuration, PPP may or may not operate on the LAN. Some configurations use PPP to set up sessions between the enterprise router and the Internet ISP, but they do not use PPP on the LAN link. Be aware that if PPP is not executed at the end-user workstation on the LAN, then the workstation cannot avail itself of the PPP services, such as authentication. That being the case, the router must act as the PPP proxy on behalf of the workstation.

The bottom part of Figure 1–1 illustrates a concept called a virtual private dial network (VPDN). An internet service provider (in the Internet "cloud" in this figure) provides all the dial-in access devices for the enterprise (modem pools, access servers, perhaps even firewalls). The enterprise need only provide a home router; modems are not needed. A connection to the service provider, such as an ATM network, provides the necessary wide area network (WAN) connection. The service provider is responsible for supporting the enterprise's city-to-city dialing needs, yet the enterprise maintains control over all locations, as well as security procedures.

The links to/from the Internet are labeled OC3, T3, and ATM in this figure. These are common user-to-Internet operations and vary depending upon individual implementation considerations. PPP can operate over all these technologies.

THE NETWORK ACCESS SERVER (NAS)

The ISP in Figure 1–1 allows the user (client) to dial-in to the network through the PSTN. The ISP usually has Network Access Servers (NAS) that sit between the user, the PSTN, and the data network (thus, the NAS is also called an edge device to the data network).

The NAS can be implemented in any kind of machine, but it is usually distinguished from a router in that it provides services on a per-user basis. A router can be configured to "tailor itself" to each user (based on an IP address), but that level of granularity is not its normal mode of operations.

Some common functions of a NAS include: (a) supporting dial-in and dial-out connections from and to users, (b) tunneling user traffic (in an encapsulation protocol) to and from other devices and networks, and (c) providing authentication, authorization, and accounting (AAA) services. The AAA services are usually in conjunction with other servers, perhaps a special security server, or an accounting server.

This book discusses the NAS operations in more detail in several of the chapters.

OPERATIONS OF A DATA LINK PROTOCOL

As we shall see in more detail later in this chapter and in Chapter 2, PPP is classified as a data link protocol. In this section, we introduce the functions of a data link protocol.

The transfer of data across the communications link between computers, terminals, and workstations must occur in a controlled and orderly manner. Since communications links experience distortions (such as noise), a method must be provided to deal with the periodic errors that result in the distortion of the data.

The data communications system must provide each workstation/ computer on the link with the capability to send data to another station, and the sending station must be assured that the data arrives error-free at the receiving station. In some systems, when the data are distorted, the receiver is able to direct the originator to resend the data.

Services must also be available to manage the traffic that is sent between the machines. Since computers have a finite amount of storage, measures must be taken to prevent one machine from sending too much data to another machine, which could result in data being lost due to the receiving machine's inability to store the data.

The system must also know how to distinguish the signals on the link that represent data from extraneous signals such as noise, and other non-data elements. The ability to determine when user data begins and when it ends is important to the proper operations of a data communications system.

Once the user traffic has arrived safely at the receiving computer, some means must be available to determine the recipient(s) of the data. After all, it does little good to undertake all the aforementioned efforts and have no procedure to pass the traffic to the proper entity (software, database, a memory buffer, etc.) at the receiving computer.

Data link protocols provide these important services. They manage the orderly flow of data across the communications path (link), and many of these protocols ensure this traffic arrives error-free at the receiving machine. They make certain data are distinguished from other signals, and they ensure data are presented to the receiving machine and a recognized application in proper order.

Figure 1–2 shows examples of data link operations on three links operating between four machines (A, B, C, D), such as workstations, routers, etc. The bottom figure shows how the data traffic is sent between nodes A and B, checked for errors, and positively acknowledged (ACK) or negatively acknowledged (NAK).

A data link protocol (also called a data link control [DLC]) operation is limited to one individual link. That is to say, link control is responsible only for the traffic between adjacent machines on a link. For example, consider a network or an internet (multiple networks connected together) where multiple communications links connect routers, networks, and other components. The data are transmitted from one node (such as router A in Figure 1–2) to the adjacent node (router B). If this node accepts the data, it may send an acknowledgment of this transmission to the originating node, after which the link control task is complete for that particular transmission. If the data are relayed to yet another node on another link, the first link's data link control is unaware of this activity. Indeed, the particular type of link protocol on *each link* within this network can be entirely different (although this approach could be costly, since the enterprise would have to train its technicians to know about types of link protocols).

The data link control protocol is usually responsible for all the transmissions on the link. For example, if a communications link has several users accessing it, the link protocol assumes the responsibility for transporting the data for all users to a receiving machine on the link.

The link protocol is generally unaware that the data on the link belongs to multiple users (if it indeed does). Most link protocols are designed so they do not know the contents of the user data that they are "transporting" to the receiving machine. Their main concern is to deliver the traffic safely from the sending to the receiving machine(s).

This concept also holds true for the user of the link protocol. The user is unaware of the activities of the link protocol; its operations usually remain transparent to the user and to the other protocols operating in the data communications system.

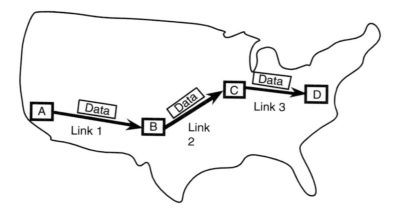

(a) Operations on three links between four machines

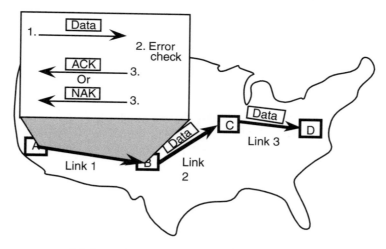

(b) A more detailed look at Link 1

Figure 1–2 Typical operations on data communications links

Eliminating ACKs, NAKs, and Retransmissions

On high-speed and/or high-quality links, the link protocol does not perform the ACKs and NAKs explained earlier, nor does it support re-transmissions. The rationale is as follows. Let us assume a one-way propagation delay of a link across the United States is about 20 ms. A T1 network transporting 53-byte ATM cells, operating at 1.544 Mbit/s would have 3,860 bytes in flight (that is, in the network) during this 20-ms interval, or about 72 cells. This load is not a big problem.[1]

However, with broadband networks operating at higher speeds, the network could have millions of bytes and thousands of cells in flight. For example, in an OC 192 network that carries ATM cell traffic, there could be 24,883,200 bytes and 469,494 cells in flight!

If the traffic may be retransmitted, the sender must hold copies of all the cells in a buffer to await the results of the error checks at the receiver. Since it takes another 20 ms or so to receive an acknowledgment, the sender's buffer must be about 50 million bytes, to accommodate for the round-trip delays (not a bad deal, if you are selling memory chips).

So, it is not practicable to perform link-layer retransmissions on high-speed links. Fortunately, most high-speed links use optical fiber, and the error rates on fiber are quite good, and an error induced by the media is not typical. PPP can be set up to either provide ACKs and NAKS or not provide them.

THE DATA LINK "HANDSHAKE"

Before communications can occur between two machines on the communications link, the data link control protocol must first establish a link connection. The term connection does not mean connection in the physical sense, because that is a matter for another protocol (at the physical layer). Indeed, the physical connection must be available before any operations can occur with a data link protocol. A link connection means that the two data link control protocols in the nodes must exchange a number of messages to establish an understanding of how the data link operations will proceed. These initial operations are known as a handshake, and are titled "Link Establishment" in Figure 1–3.

In event 1, during the handshake the protocols (depending upon the specific implementation) may negotiate a variety of options with each other, such as compression, authentication, etc.

Once the handshake is complete, the data link protocol supports the ongoing transport of traffic between the machines, shown as event 2. At

---

[1]These calculations assume the link has no overhead but the ATM cell header. For the OC n links, about 20 percent of the bandwidth is used for overhead, so the reader can reduce these figures by this amount if SONET is carrying the ATM cells in its envelope.

The figures are based on a simple calculation. Using T1 as the example: 1,544,000 × .02 (sec.)/ 8 (bits per byte) = *3860* (bytes) / 53 (bytes per cell) = 72.8 ATM cells.

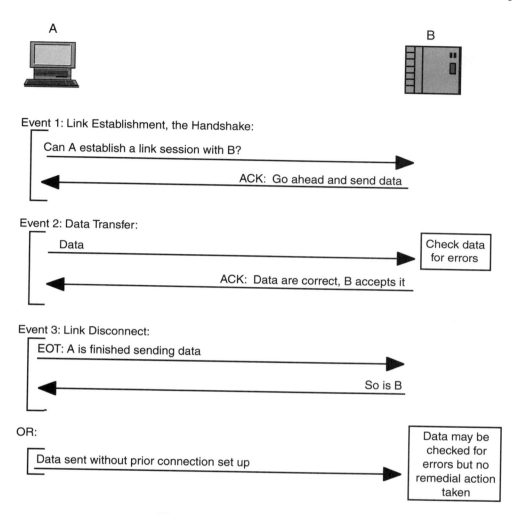

A

B

Event 1: Link Establishment, the Handshake:

Can A establish a link session with B?

ACK: Go ahead and send data

Event 2: Data Transfer:

Data

Check data
for errors

ACK: Data are correct, B accepts it

Event 3: Link Disconnect:

EOT: A is finished sending data

So is B

OR:

Data sent without prior connection set up

Data may be
checked for
errors but no
remedial action
taken

Figure 1–3   The link handshake

the end of the transmission process (event 3), either party can terminate the session with a link disconnect operation, which entails one machine sending a special link protocol signal to the other machine.

The bottom part of this figure shows another way to operate a data link protocol. This arrangement does not go through a handshake, or a termination. The procedure goes directly to a data transfer state. This approach is not common on wide area links, such as a point-to-point link, but it is widely used on LAN links such as Ethernet. PPP does not support this latter type of operation.

How PPP Fits into the Picture

PPP is somewhat of a hybrid to the link protocol operations shown in Figure 1–3. First, it may rely on another link protocol to perform these "basic" handshakes. After the initial handshake occurs, then PPP executes its own handshakes. Therefore, it is not unusual for an implementation to use two link protocols, one for initial link initialization, and PPP for further initialization and configuration operations. Chapter 2 explains this relationship in more detail.

BEYOND THE INDIVIDUAL LINK OPERATIONS: LAYER 2 TUNNELING PROTOCOL (L2TP)

Thus far the description of PPP has focused on the operations on one link only. As we will discover in subsequent chapters, because of the flexibility of PPP and because of its almost universal deployment on internet links, PPP has been extended to permit it to operate not just between two PPP peers (endpoints) on *one* link but between different devices in *separate* networks, and *multiple* links.

The ability to execute PPP procedures across multiple links and multiple networks is implemented with the Layer 2 Tunneling Protocol (L2TP). Our approach in describing L2TP, which is an instrumental tool in today's networks, will be to acquaint you with the PPP operations in the initial chapters of this book and focus on the L2TP in subsequent chapters.

THE INTERNET LAYERED ARCHITECTURE

Many of the concepts in this book are explained with the layered protocol concept. This section provides a brief review of the Internet layers.

Figure 1–4 provides a review of the Internet protocol suite layers. With some exceptions, the Open Systems Interconnection (OSI) Model layer 6 is not used. Layer 5 is not used at all.

The physical and data link layers are (as a general rule) also not defined. The philosophy is to rely on existing physical and data link systems. One notable exception to this practice is at the data link layer, where the Internet task forces have defined the PPP.

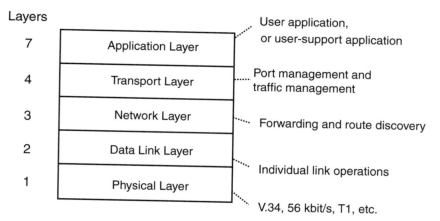

Figure 1–4   The Internet protocol suite layers

For the newcomer, here is a summary of the functions of the layers:

- *Physical layer:*   Defines the media, and physical aspects of the signals (voltages, etc.). Defines clocking and synchronization operations. Defines physical connectors. Also identified as layer 1 or L_1. Examples are T1, E1, SONET, and L_1 of Ethernet.

- *Data link layer:*   Supports the transfer of traffic over one link. May perform error detection and retransmission, depending on the specific link layer protocol. Also identified as layer 2 or L_2. Examples are PPP, LAPD, and the L_2 of Ethernet.

- *Network layer:*   Performs forwarding operations and route discovery. Supports some limited diagnostic functions, such as status reports. Also identified as network level, layer 3, or L_3. An example of forwarding is IP. An example of route discovery is Open Shortest Path First (OSPF).

- *Transport layer:*   Supports end-to-end acknowledgment of traffic, as an option. At a receiving host, supports the identification (with a port number) of the layer 7 protocol to be invoked to support incoming traffic. Also identified as layer 4 or L_4. Examples are TCP and UDP.

- *Application layer:* Contains the end user application, or another application that directly supports the end user application, such as a file transfer or an email operation. Also identified as layer 7 or L_7.

DATA LINK PROTOCOLS AND THE INTERNET MODEL

Figure 1–5 shows the relationship of the layers of the Internet layered model and specifically the relationship between the data link layer and the physical layer. The physical signals are sent between the sending data terminal equipment (DTE) and the data circuit terminating equipment (DCE), across the communications link, and then to the receiving DCE and DTE. The term DTE represents an end user machine, such as a computer,

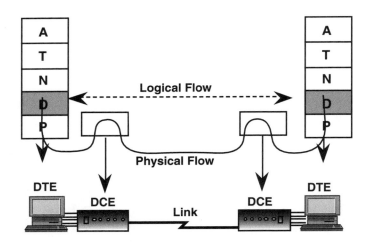

Where:
A	Application layer
T	Transport layer
N	Network layer
D	Data link layer
P	Physical layer
DTE	Data terminal equipment (user device)
DCE	Data circuit terminating equipment (modem, multiplexer, etc.)

Figure 1–5   Data link protocols and the layered model

and the term DCE represents communications gear, such as a modem, a data service unit (DSU), etc. These terms are often used in the OSI Model, but they are not used much in the Internet specifications.

The physical layer supports the exchange of traffic between all the layers in this model. For this discussion, the logical flow between the data link layers is of interest . The term logical flow means that the data link entities in both of these machines are exchanging data with each other. They are not concerned with exchanging data with any of the other layers. The dotted arrow in Figure 1–5 titled logical flow does not mean that traffic is flowing horizontally between the two layers directly (there is no such thing as etherair). Rather, it means that traffic is sent down through the physical channel (link) across the link to the receiving link protocol.

A GENERAL LOOK AT PPP OPERATIONS

This part of the chapter introduces you to the basic PPP operations and sets the stage for the more detailed discussions in subsequent chapters.

Figure 1–6 represents a summary of several key points made earlier, plus some additional information. It shows the major events involved in setting up a connection between a user and a service provider, for example, an ISP. In this example, the service provider is running a router or a Network Access Server (NAS), and the user machine is a workstation or a personal computer. Here is a description of each event depicted in the figure:

- *Event 1:* The user enters a local telephone number for the service provider. The modem dials this number. It is relayed through the local exchange carrier (LEC, not shown here) to the called party: a router serving at the service provider.
- *Event 2:* The router/NAS has a modem pool available, and one of these modems is selected for this session. It sends back a requisite answer signal to the user.
- *Event 3:* The V.90 modems[2] perform a L_1 handshake. Typical operations during this event are the agreement between the modems

---

[2]V.90 is the well-known 56 kbit/s modem that most implementators use for their analog, dial-in operations.

on a symbol rate (baud), and the bits per symbol (the bit rate in bit/s).

- *Event 4:* After the modems have finished their handshakes, the physical layer informs the data link layer that it can commence operations. This operation occurs when the L_1 carrier detect V.24 interchange circuit is turned on. Assuming the use of the Link Access Procedure for Modems (LAPM),[3] a Set Asynchronous Balanced Mode (SABM) frame is sent to the service provider. This is the initial handshake at layer 2, and most link protocols use this event to initialize the link, although LAPM may be replaced by another protocol.

- *Event 5:* The service provider returns an unnumbered acknowledgment (UA) frame to the user. The effect of the SABM and UA exchanges is to initialize the link layer. If the implementation supports retransmission operations, sequence numbers are set to 0, retransmission timers are initialized, and buffer space is reserved for the sending and reception of user traffic. Some of these operations may be set up with another exchange of frames (not shown here). They are called the exchange ID (XID) frames.

- *Event 6:* After LAPM completes its operations, PPP takes over and executes its Link Control Protocol (LCP). This protocol defines the operations for configuring the link (beyond what the SABM operation has done), and for the negotiation of options. An authentication option can be invoked, as well as a compression operation.

- *Event 7:* Next, PPP executes its Network Control Protocol (NCP) to negotiate certain options and parameters that will be used by a L_3 protocol. The IPCP (The IP Control Protocol), is an example of a specific NCP, and is used to negotiate various IP parameters, such as IP addresses.

- *Event 8:* After all the preliminary operations have been completed, the user traffic is exchanged between the user and the router/NAS.

---

[3]LAPM may not be executed. I show it here because in is found in many modems. We will see in later chapters that another L_2 protocol, LAPB, may be used in place of LAPM. Both protocols provide for sequencing, flow control and retransmission of corrupted traffic.

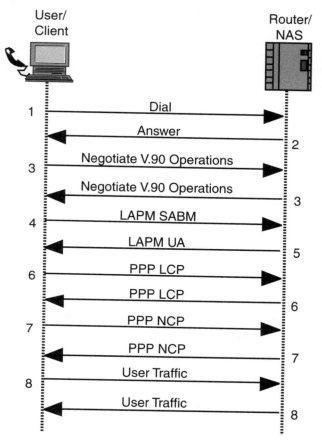

Figure 1–6   The PPP operations

This figure introduces two key PPP operations: (a) the LCP and (b) the NCP. Chapters 3 and 4 examine (respectively) these protocols.

THE PPP FAMILY

PPP is published in several Internet Request for Comments (RFC). Table 1–1 lists these RFCs. In addition, several Internet draft specifications are available that define other PPP operations. These RFCs and drafts are explained in the remaining chapters in this book.

Table 1–1   Associated RFCs

Name	RFC
Vendor extensions	2153 (Updates 1661, 1962)
Maximum receive unit	1661
Asynchronous control character map	1662
Authentication protocol	1661
Quality protocol	1661/1989
Magic Number	1661
Protocol field compression	1661
Address and control field compression	1661
FCS Alternatives	1570
Self-describing PAD	1520
Numbered Mode	1663
Multilink Procedure	1663
Call-back	1570
Connect time	Obsolete
Nominal data encapsulation	Dropped
PPP multilink protocol (MP)	1990 (Obsoletes 1717)
DCE identifier	1926
Multilink plus procedure	1934
Link discriminator	2125
LCP authentication option	Not assigned

SUMMARY

Due to its encapsulation functions and the ability to negotiate options between two machines on a communications link, PPP is the preferred link protocol used on internet dial-up links. In addition, dedicated links also use PPP. The protocol may not be used on Local Area Networks (LANs) where Ethernet and other L_2 protocols perform similar but more limited functions.

2

PPP, HDLC, and the Frames

T his chapter explains how PPP makes use of the High-Level Data Link Control (HDLC) features, such as framing and bit stuffing. In addition, PPP uses three types of HDLC frame formats to support asynchronous, octet-synchronous, and bit-synchronous traffic, which we also examine. The PPP standards for these three formats contain many rules and conventions, which are described in RFC 1662. This chapter provides a tutorial on the subject, as well as additional information on the relationships of PPP and HDLC.

HDLC

The HDLC protocol is a bit-oriented link protocol specification published by the International Standards Organization (ISO), which is summarized in the following list. For brevity, the titles are also summarized.

3309 (two documents):	HDLC frame structure and addendum
4335 (three documents):	HDLC elements of procedures
7448 (one document):	Multilink procedures (MLP)
7776 (one document):	HDLC-LAPB compatible link control procedures

7809 (five documents):   HDLC-consolidation of classes of proce-
                           dures; list of standard HDLC protocols
                           that use HDLC procedures

8471 (one document):   HDLC balanced, link address information

8885 (one document):   HDLC-additional specifications describing
                           use of an XID frame and multilink opera-
                           tions

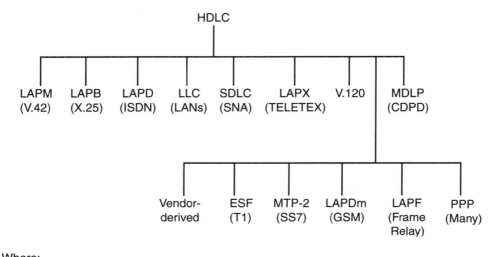

Where:
CDPD	Cellular digital packet data system
ESF	Extended super frame
GSM	Global system for mobile communications
ISDN	Integrated services digital network
LANs	Local area networks
LAPB	Link access procedure, balanced
LAPD	Link access procedure for the D channel
LAPDm	LAPD for mobile links
LAPF	LAP for frame relay
LAPM	Link access procedure for modems
LAPX	Link access procedure, half-duplex
LLC	Logical link control
MDLP	Mobile data link protocol
MTP	Message transfer port
PPP	Point-to-point protocol
SDLC	Synchronous data link control
SNA	Systems network architecture (IBM's data communications architecture)
SS7	Signaling system number 7

Figure 2–1   The High-Level Data Link Control (HDLC) "family"

HDLC has achieved wide use throughout the world. The standard provides for many functions and covers a wide range of applications. It is frequently used as a foundation for other protocols. A partial list of these protocols is depicted in Figure 2–1. The names in the parentheses identify the system or upper-layer protocol supported by the HDLC implementation option.

The PPP entry in Figure 2–1 lists many upper-layer protocols supported by PPP. As explained earlier, one of PPP's features is to transport layer 3 traffic across the point-to-point link. Due to the wide use of the Internet and intranets, the layer 3 traffic is often IP data.

RELATIONSHIP OF PPP'S OPERATIONS AND HDLC

PPP operates over HDLC, and consists of two major protocols, explained in the following material and depicted in Figure 2–2.

HDLC is often placed on circuit cards that are installed as a line card in a machine. An approach is to implement the basic functions that do not change in hardware, and load software for functions that may change or that are unique to the link protocol. For example, some of the

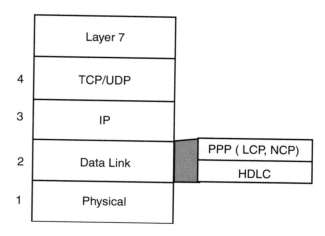

Where:
    HDLC   High-Level Data Link Control
    LCP   Link Control Protocol
    NCP   Network Control Protocol
    TCP   Transmission Control Protocol
    UDP   User Datagram Protocol

Figure 2–2   PPP and HDLC

link protocols shown in Figure 2–2 are implemented as software on an HDLC card.

The Link Control Protocol (LCP) is the first procedure that is executed when a PPP link is set up. It defines the operations for configuring the link and for negotiating options. After LCP has been executed and negotiated, authentication operations [an authentication option (AUTH)] can be invoked.

After LCP has completed its tasks, PPP uses a Network Control Protocol (NCP) to negotiate certain options and parameters that will be used by a L_3 protocol. The IPCP is an example of a specific NCP, and it is used to negotiate various IP parameters, such as IP addresses, compression, etc.

Encapsulation identifiers are placed in the PPP header to identify the type of traffic residing in the PPP information field. The NCP encapsulation identifiers are numbered x8000-BFFF, and x8021 is assigned to the IPCP. Another set of numbers identifies the specific protocol that the NCP has negotiated for use, and x0021 is used for the IP traffic. The rule for using these numbers is that the L_3 protocol identifiers are the same as negotiation protocol identifiers, less x8000.

RELATIONSHIP OF PPP TO NETWORK CONTROL PROTOCOLS (NCPs)

Figure 2–3 is another example of how other protocols can operate with PPP. The Network Control Protocols, such as X.25, IP, IPX, etc. are the conventional L_3 protocols. In some installations, these protocols operate over a compression protocol, named the Compression Control Protocol (CCP), which operates over a security protocol, called the Encryption Control Protocol (ECP). These two protocols are optional, and they are examined later. The point was made earlier that PPP operates over the core components of HDLC, as depicted in Figure 2–3.

PPP AND HDLC FORMATS

PPP supports three types of HDLC formats: (a) asynchronous HDLC (AHDLC), (b) byte-oriented HDLC (also called octet-synchronous HDLC), (c) bit-oriented HDLC (also called bit-synchronous HDLC). The most common format is bit-synchronous HDLC, but the other two are in existence.

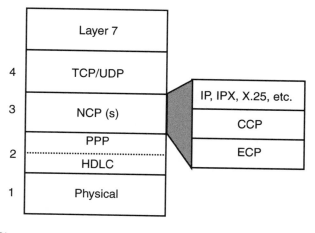

Where:
CCP	Compression Control Protocol
ECP	Encryption Control Protocol
HDLC	High Level Data Link Control
IP	Internet Protocol
IPX	Internet Packet Exchange
NCP	Network Control Protocol
PPP	Point-to-Point Protocol
TCP/UDP	Transmission Control Protocol/User Datagram Protocol

Figure 2–3   Layers above layer 2 (one example)

This section provides an overview of how these formats are created at the transmitter and interpreted at the receiver. For details, I refer you to RFC 1662, from which this overview is extracted.

Asynchronous HDLC (AHDLC)

AHLDC is used on asynchronous links that are configured with async modems and async PCs. It has some similarities to the old SLIP in that it uses special octet values to identify functions, such as x7E for frame delimiting and x7D for escape. The x7E marks the beginning of a frame and is sent between successive frames. The x7D allows the use of values x00-x1F, xFD, and x7E. The x7D is placed in front of these values.

Octet-synchronous HDLC

Octet-synchronous (RFC 1618) defines an operation for ISDN links. It is similar to AHDLC and uses the same escape and framing conventions. However, for this technique, the ASCII control characters do not have to be escaped.

Bit-synchronous HDLC

Bit-synchronous HDLC is the most common PPP format. Because it is bit-dependent, and not code- or byte-dependent, it does not need escape characters. Many of the operations are performed in hardware (on HDLC line cards). The only significant changes to the bit stream is that HDLC must check for bits in the user traffic that might be interpreted as flags at the receiver. Flags (01111110) are used by HDLC to signal the start of each frame.

HDLC is a code-transparent protocol. It does not rely on a specific code (ASCII/IA5, EBCDIC, etc.) for the interpretation of line control. For example, bit position n within a control field has a specific meaning, regardless of the other bits in the field. However, on occasion, a flag-like field, 01111110, may be inserted into the user data stream (I field) by the application process. More frequently, the bit patterns in the other fields may appear "flag-like." To prevent these "phony" flags from being inserted into the frame, HDLC provides for the transmitter to insert a zero bit after it encounters five continuous 1s anywhere between the flag of the frame and the flag of the next frame. Consequently, zero insertion applies to the address, control, information, and FCS fields. This technique is called *bit stuffing*. As the frame is stuffed, it is transmitted across the link to the receiver, where it is "unstuffed." Figure 2–4 shows these operations.

Many systems use bit stuffing and the non-return-to-zero-inverted (NRZI) encoding technique to keep the receiver clock synchronized. With NRZI, binary 1s do not cause a line transition but binary 0s do cause a change. It might appear that a long sequence of 1s could present synchronization problems since the receiver clock would not receive the line transitions necessary for the clock adjustment. However, bit stuffing en-

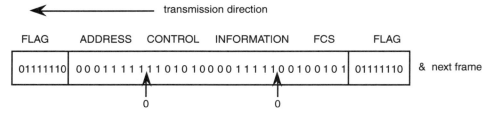

Figure 2–4   HDLC formats

sures a 0 bit exists in the data stream at least every 5 bits. The receiver can use them for clock alignment.

EXPLANATION OF TERMS

Before proceeding further, it should prove useful to define several terms, as used in the PPP specifications, and in my explanations of PPP (see Figure 2–5):

Protocol data unit (PDU): The OSI generic term to describe any unit of information, such as a datagram, a frame, or a packet.

Datagram: The PDU of the network layer (such as IP). A datagram may be encapsulated in one or more packets passed to the data link layer. A datagram contains the IP header and any traffic encapsulated into the IP data field, such as the TCP header, a layer-7 header, and data.

Packet: The basic unit of encapsulation (containing a datagram, plus header information, such as a PPP header), which is passed across the interface between the network layer and the data link layer. A packet is usually mapped to a frame; the exceptions are when data link layer fragmentation is being performed, or when multiple packets are incorporated into a single frame.

Frame: The PDU at the data link layer. A frame may include a header and/or a trailer, along with a number of protocol data units that are contained in its information (I) field.

Peer: The other end of the point-to-point link.

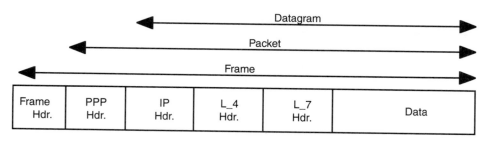

Note: Protocol data unit (PDU) describes any of these terms

Figure 2–5   Terms for PDUs

Unfortunately, some of these terms are used to describe the same type of PDU. For example, many papers and books use the terms packet and datagram interchangeably. Others use the terms packet and message (not shown here) to mean the same PDU. Still others use the terms PPP frame and PPP packet to describe what is shown in Figure 2–5 as a PPP packet.

THE PPP PDU

The PPP PDU uses the HDLC frame as stipulated in ISO 3309-1979 (and amended by ISO 3309-1984/PDAD1) and depicted in Figure 2–6. Since several parts of this book explain HDLC in detail, this material is restricted to showing the frame format and its relationship to PPP. This figure shows this format. The flag sequence is the standard HDLC flag of 01111110 (x7E), the address field is set to all 1s (Hex FF) which signifies an all-stations address. PPP does not use individual station addresses because it is a point-to-point protocol. The control field is set to identify a HDLC unnumbered information (UI) command. Its value is 00000011 (x03).

The PPP protocol field is used to identify the PDU that is encapsulated into the I field of the frame. The field values are assigned by the In-

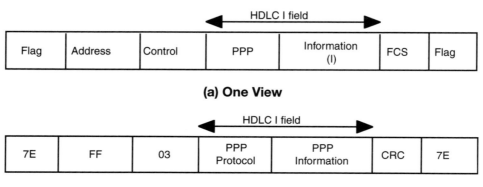

(a) One View

(b) Another View

- Flag: x7E
- HDLC address: xFF
- HDLC control: x03 (unnumbered info [UI])
- HDLC information (I) field: up to 1502 octets

Figure 2–6   The PPP frame format

ternet, and the values in the "0xxx" to "3xxx" range identify the network protocol that resides in the I field. Values in the "8xxx" to "13xxx" range identify a control protocol that is used to negotiate the protocols that will actually be used. We have more to say about this control protocol shortly.

The PPP I field contains control or user traffic, and the contents of the I field are identified by the PPP protocol field. For example, the PPP protocol field in the frame must contain hex xC021 to indicate that the I field carries Link Control Protocol (LCP) information. We will see later that there are other fields in the PP protocol field. One field is a code field (not shown). The code field can be coded to identify the type of LCP packet that is encapsulated into the frame. As examples, the code would indicate if the packet contains a configure request, which would likely be followed by a configure ACK or NAK. Additionally, the code could indicate (for example) an echo request data unit. Naturally, the next frame would probably identify the echo reply. These packets are discussed in Chapter 3.

AUTO-DETECT OPERATIONS

Although data communications did not start out with an agreed set of protocols (earlier, vendors implemented their own proprieraty systems), today it is reasonable to expect that most data communications machines operate with a standard set. Certainly, there are a wide number of features that must be known (and configured), even if the communicating parties know of the specific protocol that is to be used for the session. Nonetheless, at the link layer, a restricted set of protocols are used today. So, a productive approach is for the two communicating machines to automatically ascertain the protocol(s) that is/are to be used. This concept involves the machines examining the bits on the link (sniffing) and looking for specific bit and or timing patterns, an operation called auto-detection, see Figure 2–7.

PPP defines the procedures for auto-detecting either asynchronous or synchronous frames. Since bit-synchronous frames are the most common, we will concentrate on these operations in this discussion.

The task in most PPP implementations is for the receiver to examine the incoming bits and determine (after finding the flag) if the frame is: (a) an initial link setup frame, (b) a link control frame, or (c) a PPP frame. However, the task is more involved on some links. For example, on ISDN links, the frame may be formatted for 64 kbit/s or 65 kbit/s. Each of these implementations uses different formats.

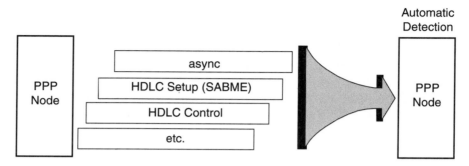

Figure 2–7   Auto-detect operations

Whatever the case may be, PPP implementations are capable of auto-detecting the incoming traffic and interpreting its format.

PPP AND ERROR CHECKING

PPP has two methods of error checking the frame at the receiver. One method discards erred frames, and the other method (an option) asks for a retransmission of the erred frame. Both operations are explained in the next two sections of this chapter. Keep in mind that PPP defaults to the first method. The retransmission method must be negotiated during the handshake.

Error Checking and Retransmission

The frame check sequence (FCS) operation is one method used by data link protocols to check for damaged bits in the received frame. The bits may be distorted by noise, crosstalk, attenuation, or other link impairments. Figure 2–8 shows this operation.

The sending site, a L_3 packet (or datagram) is sent to the data link layer. This layer adds protocol control information (PCI) on to the packet, and uses packet and PCI bits as input into a cyclic redundancy check (CRC) algorithm that computes the FCS (frame check sequence) field. This field is appended to the frame. Due to the calculation, the FCS value is dependent on the value of the PCI and packet bits. Next, flags (F) are placed around the frame and the frame is sent to the physical layer where it is sent onto the link and to the receiving station.

At this station, the frame is passed to DLC, which strips off the flags. It then performs a calculation on the PCI, the packet field, and the

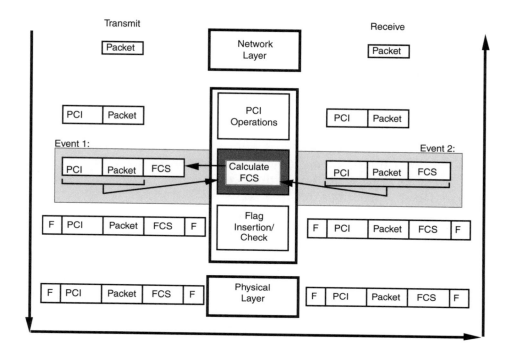

Event 1: Calculate FCS from PCI and packet bits

Event 2: (a) Calculate check value from PCI, packet, and FCS

        (b) If answer is "correct", increment V(R) variable

        (c) If answer is not "correct", do not increment V(R) variable

        (d) Next arriving frame's N(S) will not match V(R)....and

            a NAK is sent to originator

Figure 2–8   Detecting Errors, and Requesting a Retransmission (NAK)

FCS (event 2). If the answer to the calculation indicates that the frame was not damaged, it is passed up to the next DLC entity (actually, a sublayer) for further processing.

However, if the FCS calculation indicates that the frame was damaged, then (a) the frame is discarded and no other action is taken, or (b) the frame is discarded and the following occurs.

The traffic at both the transmitting and receiving sites are controlled by state variables. The transmitting site maintains a send state variable (V[S]), which is the sequence number of the next frame to be transmitted. The receiving site maintains a receive state variable (V[R]), which contains the number that is expected to be in the sequence number of the next frame. The V(S) is incremented with each frame transmitted and placed in the send sequence field [called N(S)] in the frame.

Upon receiving the frame, the receiving site checks the send sequence number with its V(R). If the CRC passes and if V(R) = N(S), it increments the variable V(R) by one, places the value in the receive sequence number field [N(R)] in a frame and sends it to the original transmitting site to complete the accountability for the transmission.

If the V(R) does not match the sending sequence number in the frame (or the CRC does not pass), an error has occurred, and NAK with a value in N(R) is sent to the original transmitting site. The N(R) value informs the transmitting DTE of the next frame that it is expected to send, i.e., the number of the frame to be retransmitted.

In the event of an error, the V(R) variable is not incremented. Therefore, when the next frame arrives (if it is correct), the frame's N(S) field will not match the V(R) variable. Consequently, the arriving traffic is considered out-of-sequence, and the DLC places the V(R) variable into the N(R) field of a frame, sets a field in the frame to indicate a NAK and sends this frame to the originator. The originator uses this frame to find out which frame is to be resent.

Error Checking but No Retransmission

Error checking but no retransmission is the default operation for PPP. The procedures just explained are used, except the variables and sequence numbers are not utilized. If the error check reveals an error, no further action is taken. Since the variables and sequence numbers are not used, it is impossible to execute retransmission operations.

SUMMARY

PPP and HDLC are L_2 partners on the data communications link. The conventional HDLC frame is used to carry the PPP payload in the HDLC information field.

While the industry has been migrating to bit-oriented procedures over the past twenty years, PPP also supports other link protocol conventions.

PPP defaults to no-retransmission operations. If sequencing, flow control, and retransmission procedures are needed, they must be negotiated during the link establishment handshake.

3

The Principal PPP Entities: LCP

This chapter examines the Link Control Protocol (LCP), the first PPP protocol to be executed. The LCP phases are discussed, as well as the state transition table, known as the finite state automaton table. The chapter concludes with an inspection of the LCP packet, the rules for the transmission of the packets, and how the PPP peer acts upon the reception of the packets.

LINK CONTROL PROTOCOL (LCP) BASICS

LCP was introduced briefly in Chapter 1. Its purpose is to support the establishment of the connection and to allow for certain configuration options to be negotiated. The protocol maintains the PPP connection and provides the procedures for terminating the connection. It also is used to set limits on the size of the packets exchanged between the parties, perform authentication, as well as detect certain errors, such as a looped-back link. In order to perform these functions, LCP (and PPP) is organized into three phases (see Box 3–1).

PPP requires that LCP be executed to open the connection between two stations before any network-layer traffic is exchanged. This requires a series of packet exchanges which are called configure packets. After

Box 3–1   The major PPP phases

Phase 1: Link establishment and configuration negotiation
Phase 2: Network Layer Protocol configuration negotiation
Phase 3: Link termination

these packets have been exchanged and a configure acknowledge packet has been sent and received between the stations, the connection is considered to be in an open state and the exchange of other packets can begin (such as NCP packets, explained in Chapter 4).

LCP confines itself only to link handshake operations. It does not understand how to negotiate the implementation of network-layer protocols. Indeed, it does not care about the upper-layer negotiations relating to the network protocols.

Link quality determination is optional and allows LCP to check to see if the link is of sufficient quality to actually bring up the network layer. A tool exists to provide an LCP echo request and an LCP echo packet. These packets are defined within the protocol and exist within the state transition tables of the protocol.

After the link establishment (and if the optional link quality determination phase is implemented), the protocol configuration allows the two stations to negotiate/configure the L_3 protocols that will be used at the network layer. This is performed by the appropriate network control protocol (NCP). The particular protocol that is used here depends on which family of NCPs is implemented.

LCP is also responsible for terminating the link connection. It is allowed to perform the termination at its discretion. Unless problems have occurred which creates this event, the link termination is usually initiated by a "housekeeping" protocol or a user-operated link control station.

THE PPP PHASES

In the process of configuring, maintaining, and terminating the PPP link, the PPP link goes through several distinct phases, shown in Figure 3–1. PPP requires that each end of the link exchange a variety of PPP packets before user traffic is exchanged. The key packets and their

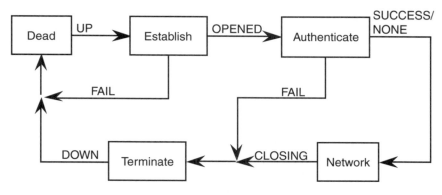

Figure 3–1   PPP phase diagram

names are introduced here and explained in more detail later. Notice that for two phases, the failure to complete them successfully results in the inability to obtain a PPP connection (the fail events in Figure 3–1).

Link Dead (physical layer not ready)

The link begins and ends with this phase. When an external event (such as a modem carrier detect signal or a network administrator configuration directive) indicates that the physical layer is ready to be used, PPP proceeds to the Link Establishment phase (shown as "Establish" in Figure 3–1). Typically, a link will return to the link dead phase automatically after the disconnection of a modem and the loss of the modem carrier, with the subsequent setting of the carrier detect bit in a register at the PPP interface. In the case of a hard-wired link, this phase may be short, but long enough to detect the presence of the device.

Link Establishment Phase

The LCP is used to establish the connection through an exchange of LCP configure packets. The LCP Opened state is entered, once an LCP Configure-ACK packet has been both sent and received. The receipt of an LCP Configure-Request packet from the PPP peer always causes a return to the Link Establishment phase from the Network-Layer Protocol phase or Authentication phase.

Once again, LCP is not concerned with configuring network layer protocols and the options within those protocols. The Network Control Protocols (NCPs) are responsible for the L_3 operations.

Authentication Phase

If an implementation desires that the peer authenticate with an authentication protocol, it requests the use of an authentication protocol during the link establishment phase. Authentication is implementation-specific, and RFC 1661 recommends that authentication occur as soon as possible after the completion of the link establishment phase.

If this phase fails, the authenticator (the challenging party) proceeds directly to the termination phase to terminate the physical layer signals as soon as possible.

Only three packet types are permitted during the authentication phase: (a) LCP, (b) authentication, and (c) link quality monitoring. All other packets are discarded without further actions (they are silently discarded).

Network-Layer Protocol Phase

Next, each network-layer protocol (such as IP, IPX, or AppleTalk) is separately configured by the appropriate Network Control Protocol (NCP) (shown as "Network" in Figure 3–1). After a NCP has reached the Opened state, PPP will carry the corresponding network-layer protocol packets. During this phase, link traffic consists of any possible combination of LCP, NCP, and network-layer protocol packets that are supported in the specific PPP implementation. Otherwise, unsupported network-layer traffic is silently discarded.

Link Termination Phase

LCP is used to close the link through an exchange of terminate packets. When the link is closing, PPP informs the network-layer protocols so that they may take appropriate action. After the exchange of terminate packets, the physical layer is usually notified to disconnect. Likewise, if the network layer has been established through NCP, the network-layer protocols should be notified so that they may take any appropriate actions.

The sender of the LCP Terminate-Request packet does not disconnect until it has received the LCP Terminate-ACK packet. A restart timer is invoked during this operation; the sender of the Terminate-ACK waits for the Terminate-ACK, or waits until the restart timer has expired before disconnecting. Likewise, the receiver of the Terminate-Request packet sends the Terminate-ACK and then waits at least one restart timer before disconnecting.

Use of Timers During the Authentication and Network Layer Phases

RFC 1661 provides guidelines on the use of timers during the LCP operations. This section is a brief summary of these guidelines.

Due to the variable times it may take to complete the authentication and network-layer phases, a PPP implementation should not use timers or retries which discourage variable-length operations, as well as re-transmissions. However, PPP should be flexible during these phases, but should not (especially in the authentication phase) give the challenged party unlimited retrys to be authenticated.

PPP uses a restart timer to time the sending of LCP Configure-Request and Terminate-Request packets. After either of these packets are sent, the timer is turned on, and its expiration will result in the re-transmission of the original packet. The receipt of an ACK for the packet turns off the Restart timer.

INTRODUCTION TO THE OPTIONS

The PPP options are many and varied, and are described in subsequent parts of this book. The use of specific options will be determined by the needs of the enterprise. For example, an IBM-based enterprise will need to negotiate different options than an Apple-based enterprise. Notwithstanding, most LCP systems support at least the following options:

- Authentication (PPP option 3)
- Link Quality Monitoring (PPP option 4)
- Magic Number (PPP option 5)

For this part of the book, we concentrate on how LCP negotiates options, and later we will examine the options themselves.

The PPP Option Negotiation Automaton

To govern the operations of PPP in a more detailed manner than the general phase diagram (shown in Figure 3–1), PPP also defines a finite-state automaton table. Table 3–1 defines (a) events, (b) actions, and (c) state transitions of the finite-state automaton. Events are reception of PPP packets from the peer, expiration of the restart timer, and the recep-

Table 3–1 The Finite-state Automaton Table [RFC 1661]

Events	State 0 Initial	State 1 Starting	State 2 Closed	State 3 Stopped	State 4 Closing	State 5 Stopping	State 6 Req-Sent	State 7 ACK-Rcvd	State 8 ACK-Sent	State 9 Opened
Up	2	irc,scr/6	—	—	—	—	—	—	—	—
Down	—	—	0	tls/1	0	1	1	1	1	tld/1
Open	tls/1	1	irc,scr/6	3r	5r	5r	6	7	8	9r
Close	0	tlf/0	2	2	4	4	irc,str/4	irc,str/4	irc,str/4	tld,irc,str/4
TO+	—	—	—	—	str/4	str/5	scr/6	scr/6	scr/8	—
TO-	—	—	—	—	tlf/2	tlf/3	tlf/3p	tlf/3p	tlf/3p	—
RCR+	—	—	sta/2	irc,scr,sca/8	4	5	sca/8	sca,tlu/9	sca/8	tld,scr,sca/8
RCR-	—	—	sta/2	irc,scr,sca/8	4	5	scn/6	scn/7	scn/6	tld,scr,scn/6
RCA	—	—	sta/2	sta/3	4	5	irc/7	scr/6x	irc,tlu/9	tld,scr/6x
RCN	—	—	sta/2	sta/3	4	5	irc,scr/6	scr/6x	irc,scr/8	tld,scr/6x
RTR	—	—	sta/2	sta/3	sta/4	sta/5	sta/6	sta/6	sta/6	tld,scr,sta/5
RTA	—	—	2	3	tlf/2	tlf/3	6	6	8	tld,scr/6
RUC	—	—	scj/2	scj/3	scj/4	scj/5	scj/6	scj/7	scj/8	scj/9
RXJ+	—	—	2	3	4	5	6	6	8	9
RXJ-	—	—	tlf/2	tlf/3	tlf/2	tlf/3	tlf/3	tlf/3	tlf/3	tld,irc,str/5
RXR	—	—	2	3	4	5	6	7	8	ser/9

Box 3–2   Terms Used in Table 3–1 [RFC1661]

```
Events                                    Actions

Up    = lower layer is Up                 tlu = This-Layer-Up
Down  = lower layer is Down               tld = This-Layer-Down
Open  = administrative Open               tls = This-Layer-Started
Close = administrative Close              tlf = This-Layer-Finished

TO+   = Timeout with counter > 0          irc = Initialize-Restart-Count
TO-   = Timeout with counter expired      zrc = Zero-Restart-Count

RCR+  = Receive-Configure-Request (Good)  scr = Send-Configure-Request
RCR-  = Receive-Configure-Request (Bad)
RCA   = Receive-Configure-ACK             sca = Send-Configure-ACK
RCN   = Receive-Configure-NAK/Rej         scn = Send-Configure-Nak/Rej

RTR   = Receive-Terminate-Request         str = Send-Terminate-Request
RTA   = Receive-Terminate-ACK             sta = Send-Terminate-ACK

RUC   = Receive-Unknown-Code              scj = Send-Code-Reject
RXJ+  = Receive-Code-Reject (permitted)
        or Receive-Protocol-Reject
RXJ-  = Receive-Code-Reject (catastrophic)
        or Receive-Protocol-Reject
RXR   = Receive-Echo-Request              ser = Send-Echo-Reply
        or Receive-Echo-Reply
        or Receive-Discard-Request
```

tion of commands from a managing entity at the peer. Transitions and actions are caused by events.

Table 3–1 shows the states across the table, and the events as rows in the table. The entries within the table are state transitions and actions in the form: action(s)/new-state. Multiple actions may occur and are separated with commas. A dash in the table means an illegal transition. The terms in Table 3–1 are described Box 3–2.

ANOTHER LOOK AT THE LAYERED ARCHITECTURE

Figure 3–2 shows the PPP layered architecture, and introduces several new concepts. A managing entity, depicted in Figure 3–2 as layer management or provisioning protocol, might be acting on behalf of a

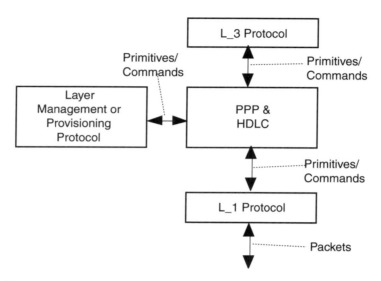

**Figure 3–2   Possible interfaces for evoking the option nego-
tiation automaton**

vendor-supplied provisioning protocol (or a network management protocol, such as the Simple Network Management Protocol (SNMP), that interworks with the layer management entity). The primitives/commands
that operate between the layers are implemented with C function calls,
system library calls, etc. For this discussion, I will use the term "administrator" to identify the implementor of the primitives/commands.

A simple explanation of how this model functions is as follows: Let
us assume that the two PPP peers have established a connection, and are
in an "Opened" state. The administrator decides that the link connection
should be terminated, and issues a "Close" primitive through layer management to PPP. PPP's job is to send a termination packet to its peer and
a primitive to its upper layer to signal that PPP is "Down."

The primitives/commands are valuable tools for software designers.
They provide a framework for coding application programming interfaces
(APIs) into the PPP software.

PPP STATES, EVENTS, AND ACTIONS

The PPP state transition table used by itself is not a model of clar-
ity. When I first began using it, I found myself circling back and forth between the states, and unable to get to the closed and stop states for the

two peers. The reason is that the table should not be read by itself. It should be studied along with the explanations of the states, events, and actions, which I failed to do initially. To that end, the next three sections of this chapter provide a summary of these parts of the state table, which I have extracted from RFC 1661. Be aware that these explanations are summaries, and RFC 1661 should be studied for the more detailed rules.

States

Initial state: In this state, the lower layer is unavailable (Down), and no Open has been given to PPP by the administrator. The Restart timer is not running yet.

Starting state: This state is the Open counterpart to the Initial state. An Open has been initiated, but the lower layer is still not operating. The Restart timer is not running. When the physical layer comes up, a Configure-Request packet is sent to the peer.

Closed state: The link is now Up, but no Open has occurred. The Restart timer is not running. During this state, Configure-Request packets are not allowed, and will be silently discarded, and the peer sent a Terminate-ACK packet.

Stopped state: This state is the Open counterpart to the Closed state. It is entered when the automaton is waiting for a Down event after the This-Layer-Finished action, or after sending a Terminate-ACK. The Restart timer is not running. This state accepts Configure-Request packets, but it does not accept others. RFC 1661 provides a helpful description of the reasons for implementing the Stopped state, as well as an implementation option. I quote directly from RFC 1661:

> The Stopped state is a junction state for link termination, link configuration failure, and other automaton failure modes. These potentially separate states have been combined. There is a race condition between the Down event response (from the This-Layer-Finished action) and the Receive-Configure-Request event. When a Configure-Request arrives before the Down event, the Down event will supercede by returning the automaton to the Starting state. This prevents attack by repetition.
>
> After the peer fails to respond to Configure-Requests, an implementation MAY wait passively for the peer to send Configure-Requests. In this case, the This-Layer-Finished action is not used for the TO- event in states Req-Sent, Ack-Rcvd and Ack-Sent.

Closing state: To move to this state, a Terminate-Request packet has been sent to the peer, the Restart timer is running, and the sending peer is awaiting a Terminate-ACK.

According to RFC 1661:

> Upon reception of a Terminate-Ack, the Closed state is entered. Upon the expiration of the Restart timer, a new Terminate-Request is transmitted, and the Restart timer is restarted. After the Restart timer has expired Max-Terminate times, the Closed state is entered.

Stopping state: This state is the Open counterpart to the Closing state. A Terminate-Request has been sent and the Restart timer is running, but a Terminate-ACK has not yet been received. The idea of this state is to provide a means to terminate completely a link session before sending any more traffic. The link can then be reconfigured with the Stopped or Starting states.

Request-Sent state: In this state a peer is trying to configure the connection; it has sent a Configure-Request packet, has started the Restart timer, and is awaiting a Configure-ACK packet.

ACK-Received state: In this state, the Configure-Request has been sent, and ACKed; the Restart timer is running because the Configure-ACK has not yet been sent.

ACK-Sent state: In this state, the Configure-Request and Configure-ACK packets have been sent, but a Configure-Ack has not yet been received. The Restart timer is still running, since a Configure-Ack has not yet been received. Remember that the handshake between the peers requires both parties to exchange the request and ACK packets.

Opened state: In this state, the peer has sent and received the Configure-ACK packets.

Events

Up Event: This event occurs when the physical layer is connected and so indicates to PPP. For example, the modems have finished their negotiations and have raised the carrier detect signal.[1] The Up Event is

---

[1] The manner in which the physical layer notifies the data link layer about its operations can be performed through registers on the line card at the physical interface. For example, in a modem dial-up arrangement, a modem status register is also used to control the interchange circuits between the modem and the user device, say a personal computer (PC). The PC port uses this register for the following tasks:
  - enables/disables request-to-send (RTS) lead
  - enables/disables clear-to-send (CTS) lead
  - indication that modem has detected a ringing signal
  - indication that a ringing signal is no longer on the line
  - indication that modem has detected a carrier signal on the line

also used by LCP to signal each NCP that the link is entering the Network-Layer Protocol phase.

Down Event: This event occurs when the physical layer indicates that it is no longer able to transport traffic. For example, it can occur if the modem's signals deteriorate, and the carrier detect signal and carrier detect bit in the modem status register is turned off. It is also used by the LCP to notify each NCP that PPP is leaving the Network-Layer Protocol Phase.

Open Event: The administrator uses this event to indicate that the link is able to carry traffic. It does not mean the link is Opened, but that configuration operations are allowed to begin. If for any reason the link becomes unavailable, RFC 1661 requires that the automaton progress to a state where the link is ready to reopen.

Once again, RFC 1661 provides some useful information on the Open Event, and I quote directly from the RFC:

> Experience has shown that users will execute an additional Open command when they want to renegotiate the link. This might indicate that new values are to be negotiated.
>
> Since this is not the meaning of the Open event, it is suggested that when an Open user command is executed in the Opened, Closing, Stopping, or Stopped states, the implementation issue a Down event, immediately followed by an Up event. Care must be taken that an intervening Down event cannot occur from another source.
>
> The Down followed by an Up will cause an orderly renegotiation of the link, by progressing through the Starting to the Request-Sent state. This will cause the renegotiation of the link, without any harmful side effects.

Close Event: This event indicates that the link is not available for traffic. A provisioning protocol, layer management, or the L_3 protocol (shown in Figure 3–2) has indicated that the link is not allowed to be Opened. If the link is not in the Closed state when the Open event occurs, the automaton attempts to terminate the connection. A new Open event must occur before a link reconfiguration can occur.

Timeout (TO+, TO–) Event: This event indicates the expiration of the Restart timer. The Restart timer is used to time responses to Configure-Request and Terminate-Request packets.

The TO+ event indicates that the Restart counter is greater than zero, which triggers the Configure-Request or Terminate-Request packet to be retransmitted. The TO– event indicates that the Restart counter is not greater than zero, resulting in the cessation of packet retransmittal.

Receive-Configure-Request (RCR+, RCR–) Event: This event occurs when a Configure-Request packet is received from the peer. The

Configure-Request packet indicates the need to open a connection and may specify Configuration Options. The RCR+ event indicates that the Configure-Request was acceptable. As a result, a Configure-ACK packet is transmitted. The RCR– event indicates that the Configure-Request was unacceptable. As a result, a Configure-NAK or Configure-Reject packet is returned to the peer.

Receive-Configure-ACK (RCA) Event: This event occurs when a valid Configure-ACK packet is received from the peer, which is a positive response to a Configure-Request packet.

Receive-Configure-NAK/Rej (RCN) Event: This event occurs when a valid Configure-NAK or Configure-Reject packet is received from the peer, and these packets are negative responses to a Configure-Request packet.

Receive-Terminate-Request (RTR) Event: This event occurs when a Terminate-Request packet is received, which indicates the desire of the peer to close the connection. This event is not the same as the Close event, and does not override any Open command emanating from the local provisioning protocol (again, see Figure 3–2).

Receive-Terminate-Ack (RTA) Event: This event occurs when a Terminate-ACK packet is received from the peer, which is usually in response to a Terminate-Request packet. The Terminate-ACK packet may also indicate that the peer is in Closed or Stopped states. It resynchronizes the link configuration.

Receive-Unknown-Code (RUC) Event: This event occurs when an uninterpretable packet is received from the peer. A Code-Reject packet is sent back to the peer.

Receive-Code-Reject, Receive-Protocol-Reject (RXJ+, RXJ–) Events: These events occur when a Code-Reject or a Protocol-Reject packet is received from the peer. RXJ+ occurs when a rejected code is within the scope of the PPP operation, and informs the offending peer not to send the packet type again. RXJ– occurs when the rejected code results in an unrecoverable error and terminates the connections.

Receive-Echo-Request, Receive-Echo-Reply, Receive-Discard-Request (RXR) Events: These events occur when an Echo-Request, Echo-Reply or Discard-Request packet is received from the peer. The Echo-Reply packet is a response to an Echo-Request packet. There is no reply to an Echo-Reply or Discard-Request packet.

This concludes the overview of the events, which should be sufficient for our general description. Once again, RFC 1661 should be studied for more details, and some very helpful implementation notes.

Actions

The actions in the automaton are caused by events and usually indicate the transmission of packets and/or the starting or stopping of the Restart timer.

Illegal-Event (–) Action: This action indicates an event that cannot occur in the automaton. The implementation has an internal error, which should be reported and logged. No transition is taken, and the implementation does not reset or freeze.

This-Layer-Up (tlu) Action: This action informs the upper layers or a provisioning layer that the automaton is entering the Opened state, and it is used by the LCP to signal the Up event to the NCP, or provisioning protocol. It may also be used by the NCP to indicate that the link is available for its network-layer traffic.

This-Layer-Down (tld) Action: This action indicates to the upper layers or a provisioning layer that the automaton is leaving the Opened state. This action is used by the LCP to signal the Down event to a NCP, authentication protocol, or link quality protocol. It may be used by the NCP to indicate that the link is no longer available for its network layer traffic.

This-Layer-Started (tls) Action: This action indicates to the lower layers that the automaton is entering the Starting state, and the lower layer (L_1) is needed for the link. The lower layer responds with an Up event when the lower layer is available.

This-Layer-Finished (tlf) Action: This action indicates to the lower layers that the automaton is entering the Initial, Closed, or Stopped states, and the lower layer is no longer needed for the link. The lower layer responds with a Down event when the lower layer has terminated.

Initialize-Restart-Count (irc) Action: This action sets the Restart counter to the appropriate value (Max-Terminate or Max-Configure). The counter is decremented for each transmission, including the first.

Zero-Restart-Count (zrc) Action: This action sets the Restart counter to zero and allows the automaton to pause before proceeding to the needed final state.

Send-Configure-Request (scr) Action: With this action, a Configure-Request packet is transmitted. This indicates the need to open a connection with a specified set of Configuration Options. The Restart timer is started when the Configure-Request packet is transmitted, to guard against packet loss. The Restart counter is decremented each time a Configure-Request is sent.

Send-Configure-ACK (sca) Action: With this action, a Configure-ACK packet is transmitted, which acknowledges the reception of a Configure-Request packet with an acceptable set of Configuration Options.

Send-Configure-NAK (scn) Action: This action entails sending a Configure-NAK or Configure-Reject packet, as appropriate. This negative response reports the reception of a Configure-Request packet with an unacceptable set of Configuration Options. The Configure-NAK packets refuse a Configuration Option value and also suggest an acceptable value. In contrast, Configure-Reject packets refuse all negotiations regarding any options.

Send-Terminate-Request (str) Action: This action entails the sending of a Terminate-Request packet and is used to inform the peer that the sender wishes to close a connection. The restart timer is used for this operation.

Send-Terminate-ACK (sta) Action: A Terminate-ACK packet is transmitted with this action. This action acknowledges the reception of a Terminate-Request packet or otherwise serves to synchronize the automaton.

Send-Code-Reject (scj) Action: A Code-Reject packet is transmitted with this action. The action indicates the reception of an unknown type of packet.

Send-Echo-Reply (ser) Action: An Echo-Reply packet is transmitted with this action. The action acknowledges the reception of an Echo-Request packet.

THE LCP INFORMATION

In Chapter 2, we examined the general structure of the PPP protocol data unit and its relationship to HDLC. Figure 3–3 extends this examination with a more detailed look at the fields that are encapsulated into the PPP information field for the LCP operation.

The protocol number for LCP is xC021, and the contents of the remainder of the information field are a function of the code field. For LCP, the code field value identifies a Configure-Request message, Configure-ACK message, etc. The ID field is used to match and coordinate request messages to their associated response messages. The length field defines the length (in octets) of the entire information field.

Thereafter, the remainder of the information field is propagated with options. This field is coded with two or three values: (a) Type-

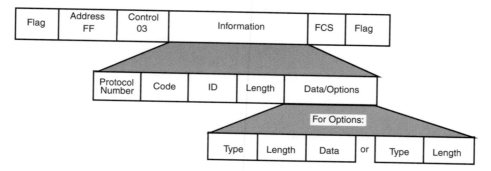

Figure 3–3   Negotiation message format

Length-Data, or (b) Type-Length. The options field is used between the PPP nodes to inform each other about their desires and capabilities. It is explained in more detail later.

THE LCP PACKETS

This section describes the LCP packets. These packets are classified as follows:

- *Link Configuration packets* are used to establish and configure a link (Configure-Request, Configure-ACK, Configure-NAK and Configure-Reject).
- *Link Termination packets* are used to terminate a link (Terminate-Request and Terminate-ACK).
- *Link Maintenance packets* are used to manage and debug a link (Code-Reject, Protocol-Reject, Echo-Request, Echo-Reply, and Discard-Request).

Each Configuration Option specifies a default value. This ensures that LCP packets are always recognizable, even when one end of the link mistakenly believes the link to be open. Exactly one LCP packet is encapsulated in the PPP Information field, where the PPP protocol number indicates protocol xC021 (Link Control Protocol).

The overall Link Control Protocol packet format is shown in Figure 3–4. The fields are transmitted from left to right.

0	1-6	7	8	9-14	1 5	16-30	3 1
	Code			Identifier		Length	
Data							

Note: Numbers at the top of the figure are the bit positions of the fields

Figure 3–4   Format of LCP packet

The fields in this packet are:

- *Code field*: Identifies the kind of LCP packet:
  - 1   Configure-Request
  - 2   Configure-ACK
  - 3   Configure-NAK
  - 4   Configure-Reject
  - 5   Terminate-Request
  - 6   Terminate-ACK
  - 7   Code-Reject
  - 8   Protocol-Reject
  - 9   Echo-Request
  - 10   Echo-Reply
  - 11   Discard-Request
- *Identifier:* Used in matching requests and replies.
- *Length:* Indicates the length of the LCP packet, including the Code, Identifier, Length and Data fields. The length field performs this same type of function in all LCP packets and therefore is not discussed further.
- *Data:* Format of the Data field is determined by the Code field. It contains options, error codes, user data and other values described in the next sections

Before we examine the LCP packets in detail, let us take another look at a packet exchange between two PPP peers, shown in Figure 3–5, as peer A and peer B. The events show that both peers send Configure-Request packets because each is setting up the options it wants its peer to support. So, the negotiated options need not be the same in each direction.

The configure-NAK packet sent from peer B to peer A (event 2) is used to inform peer A that peer B would prefer to modify one or more of the negotiation parameters that were in the Configure-Request packet in event 1. It is assumed in event 3 that peer A accedes to peer B's "hint"

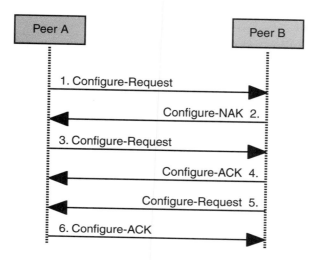

Figure 3–5   Typical PPP handshake

and changes the parameters in event 3. In event 4, peer B accepts the handshake from peer A. Events 5 and 6 complete the handshake from the peer B-to-peer A standpoint.

Figure 3–6 shows the use of the Configure-Reject packet (event 2). In this situation, peer B tells peer A that one or more configuration options in event 1 are not recognizable (not understood). In event 3, peer A takes remedial action and its revised request is ACKed in event 4.

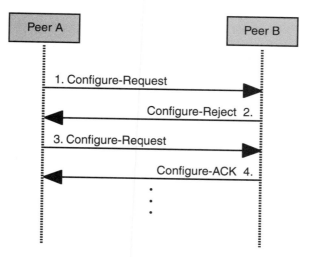

Figure 3–6   Rejecting the options

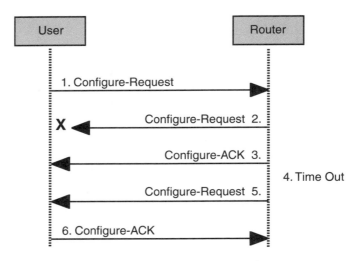

Figure 3–7   Error recovery by PPP

Error Recovery

The LCP has a method to recover from errors. In Figure 3–7, the two PPP nodes are in the negotiation phase, and both have issued Configure-Request messages to each other. However, the message from the router does not arrive at the user node in a manner that allows it to be interpreted. Therefore, the LCP module at the router times-out and resends the message.

What triggers the retransmission? The router (or any node that sends the message) starts a timer upon sending the Configure-Request message. It expects its peer to return a Configure-ACK. Since the user node did not receive the message, it has no way to send this ACK, so the router simply resends the message after the timer has expired.

Link Configuration Packets

Refer back to Figure 3–4, as the same format is used for all the Configure packets. For the Configure-Request, a node opens a connection by transmitting a Configure-Request packet. The Options field is filled with any desired changes to the link defaults. Configuration Options are not included with default values. The fields are transmitted from left to right. The fields in this packet are:

- *Code:* 1 for Configure Request

- *Identifier:* The Identifier field is changed when the contents of the Options field changes, and whenever a valid reply has been received for a previous request.

- *Options:* This field contains a list of zero or more Configuration Options that the sender wishes to negotiate. All Configuration Options are negotiated simultaneously.

Configure-ACK Packet. When every Configuration Option received in the Configure-Request packet is recognizable and all the values are acceptable, then the node transmits a Configure-ACK. The acknowledged Configuration Options cannot be reordered or modified, because the sender is expecting the order to remain the same.

The Identifier field in this packet must match that of the last transmitted Configure-Request. Additionally, the Configuration Options in a Configure-ACK must match those of the last transmitted Configure-Request.

The fields in this packet are:

- *Code:* 2 for Configure-ACK
- *Identifier:* This field is a copy of the Identifier field of the Configure-Request packet.
- *Options:* This field contains the list of zero or more Configuration Options that the sender is acknowledging. All Configuration Options are acknowledged simultaneously.

Configure-NAK Packet. If all the received Configuration Options are recognizable, but some values are not acceptable, the receiving node transmits a Configure-NAK. The Options field is filled with the unacceptable Configuration Options from the Configure-Request. Therefore, *all acceptable* Configuration Options are filtered out of the Configure-NAK. In keeping with the overall protocol, the Configuration Options from the Configure-Request must not be reordered.

Another rule of RFC 1661 is that an implementation may be configured to request the negotiation of a specific Configuration Option. If that option is not listed, then that option can be appended to the list of NAKed Configuration Options, in order to prompt the peer to include that option in its next Configure-Request packet.

The reception of a valid Configure-NAK indicates that when a new Configure-Request is sent, the Configuration Options may be modified as specified in the Configure-NAK.

The fields in this packet are:

- *Code:* 3 for Configure-NAK.
- *Identifier:* This field is a copy of the Identifier field of the Configure-Request which caused this Configure-NAK packet.
- *Options:* This field contains this list of zero or more Configure Options that the sender is NAK'ing. All Configuration Options are always NAKed simultaneously.

Configure-Reject Packet. If some Configuration Options received in a Configure-Request are not recognizable or are not acceptable for negotiation, the receiving node transmits a Configure-Reject. The Options field is filled only with the unacceptable Configuration Options from the Configure-Request. All recognizable and negotiable Configuration Options are filtered out of the Configure-Reject. The Configuration Options cannot be reordered or modified.

The Identifier field of the Configure-Reject must match that of the last transmitted Configure-Request. Also, the Configuration Options in a Configure-Reject must be a proper subset of those in the last transmitted Configure-Request.

The Reception of a valid Configure-Reject indicates that when a new Configure-Request is sent, it does not include any of the Configuration Options listed in the Configure-Reject.

The fields for this packet are:

- *Code:* 4 for Configure-Reject
- *Identifier:* This field is a copy of the Identifier field of the Configure-Request which caused this Configure-Reject packet.
- *Options:* This field contains the list of zero or more Configuration Options that the sender is rejecting. All Configuration Options are rejected simultaneously

Link Termination Packets

Figure 3–8 shows the format for the Terminate-Request and Terminate-ACK packets. Terminate-Request and Terminate-ACK packets are used by LCP to provide a mechanism for closing a connection, and a node transmits a Terminate-Request to initiate the close. Terminate-Request packets continue to be sent until: (a) Terminate-ACK is received, (b) the lower layer indicates that it has gone down, or (c) a sufficiently large

0	1-6	7	8	9-14	1 5	16-30	3 1
	Code			Identifier		Length	
Data							

Note: Numbers at the top of the figure are the bit positions of the fields

Figure 3–8 The Terminate-Request and Terminate-ACK packets

number have been transmitted such that the peer is down with reasonable certainty.

The Terminate-ACK packet is to be transmitted in response to the Terminate-Request packet. The reception of a solicited Terminate-ACK packet indicates that the peer is in the Closed or Stopped states, or is in need of re-negotiation.

The fields in this packet are:

- *Code:* 5 for Terminate-Request, and 6 for Terminate-ACK.
- *Identifier:* On transmission, this field is changed whenever the content of the Data field changes, and whenever a valid reply has been received for a previous request. For retransmissions, the Identifier field can remain unchanged. On reception, the Identifier field of the Terminate-Request is copied into the Identifier field of the Terminate-ACK packet.
- *Data:* This field contains uninterpreted data for use by the sender.

Code-Reject Packet. The reception of an LCP packet with an unknown Code indicates that the peer is operating with a different version of PPP. This situation is reported back to the sender of the unknown Code by transmitting a Code-Reject packet (see Figure 3–9). RFC 1661 suggests that, upon reception of the Code-Reject of an important code, the node should report the problem and drop the connection, since it is unlikely that the situation can be rectified automatically.

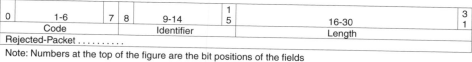

0	1-6	7	8	9-14	1 5	16-30	3 1
	Code			Identifier		Length	
Rejected-Packet							

Note: Numbers at the top of the figure are the bit positions of the fields

Figure 3–9 The Code-Reject packet

The fields in this packet are:

- *Code:* 7 for Code-Reject.
- *Identifier:* This field is changed for each Code-Reject sent.
- *Rejected Packet:* This field contains a copy of the LCP packet which is being rejected. It begins with the Information field and does not include any data-link layer headers nor an FCS.

Protocol-Reject Packet.   The reception of a PPP packet with an unknown Protocol field indicates that the peer is attempting to use a protocol that is unsupported. This situation usually occurs when the peer attempts to configure a new protocol. If the LCP automaton is in the Opened state, then this situation is reported back to the peer by transmitting a Protocol-Reject. Upon reception of a Protocol-Reject (see Figure 3–10), the peer stops sending packets of the indicated protocol at the earliest opportunity.

A rule imposed by RFC 1661 is that the Protocol-Reject packets can only be sent in the LCP Opened state. Protocol-Reject packets received in any state other than the LCP Opened state are to be silently discarded.

The fields in this packet are:

- *Code:* 8 for Protocol-Reject.
- *Identifier:* This field is changed for each Protocol-Reject sent.
- *Rejected-Protocol:* This field contains the PPP Protocol field of the rejected packet.
- *Rejected-Information:* This field contains a copy of the rejected packet. It begins with the Information field, and does not include any data-link layer headers nor an FCS.

Link Maintenance Packets

Echo packets.   Figure 3–11 shows the Echo-Request and Echo-Reply packets, which are Link Maintenance packets. The LCP includes Echo-Request and Echo-Reply packets in order to provide a link-layer

0	1-6	7	8	9-14	1 5	16-30	3 1
Code			Identifier			Length	
Rejected-Protocol					Rejected-Information . . .		

Note: Numbers at the top of the figure are the bit positions of the fields

Figure 3–10   The Protocol-Reject packet

0	1-6	7	8	9-14	1 5	16-30	3 1
	Code			Identifier		Length	
				Magic-Number			
Data							

Note: Numbers at the top of the figure are the bit positions of the fields

Figure 3–11   The Echo-Request and Echo-Reply packet

loopback mechanism for use in exercising both directions of the link. Upon reception of an Echo-Request in the LCP Opened state, an Echo-Reply must be transmitted, and these packets can only be sent in the LCP Opened State.

The fields in this packet are:

- *Code:* 9 for Echo-Request, and 10 for Echo-Reply
- *Identifier:* On transmission, this field is changed whenever the content of the Data field changes, and whenever a valid reply has been received for a previous request. On reception, the Identifier field of the Echo-Request is copied into the Identifier field of the Echo-Reply packet.
- *Magic-Number:* This field aids in detecting links which are in the looped-back condition. Until the Magic-Number Configuration Option has been successfully negotiated, the Magic-number must be transmitted as zero.
- *Data:* This field contains uninterpreted data for use by the sender.

Discard-Request Packet.   The LCP includes a Discard-Request packet (see Figure 3–12) in order to provide a link-layer sink mechanism for use in exercising the local-to-remote direction of the link.

The Discard-Request packets are sent only in the LCP Opened state. On reception, the receiver must silently discard any Discard-Request that it receives.

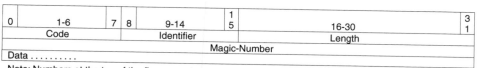

0	1-6	7	8	9-14	1 5	16-30	3 1
	Code			Identifier		Length	
				Magic-Number			
Data							

Note: Numbers at the top of the figure are the bit positions of the fields

Figure 3–12   The Discard-Request packet

The fields in this packet are:

- *Code:* 11 for Discard-Request
- *Identifier:* This field is changed for each Discard-Request sent.
- *Magic-Number:* This field is four octets and aids in detecting links which are in the looped-back condition. Until the Magic-Number Configuration Option has been successfully negotiated, the Magic-Number is transmitted as zero.
- *Data:* This field contains uninterpreted data for use by the sender.

SUMMARY

The LCP is the basic bootstrapping protocol for PPP. It is invoked after the physical connection is established between the PPP peers. The principal task of LCP is to initialize the link layer between the two nodes and exchange the necessary packets for these nodes to negotiate a variety of options. After LCP has performed its duties, the baton is passed to another PPP protocol, a Network Control Protocol (NCP) in order to initialize and negotiate the network layer (L_3) operations between the PPP peers.

4

The Principal PPP Entities: NCP

T he focus of this chapter is on Network Control Protocols (NCP). There are multiple NCPs, one for each network (L_3) protocol, and for some L_2 LAN protocols. The emphasis in this chapter is on the Internet Protocol Control Protocol (IPCP), and how a dial-in client is assigned an IP address by a server. The last part of the chapter provides a summary of other NCPs.

PURPOSE OF NCP

The job of the NCP is set up a L_3 protocol and then negotiate specific options pertaining to the protocol. In some situations, the operations do not entail negotiations as much as an assignment of options from one machine to the next.

To distinguish between the NCP operations to support a network protocol and the operations of the actual network protocol itself, two PPP protocol numbers are assigned. For NCP traffic, the PPP protocol number ranges between x8000 and xBFFF. For the network protocol (which carries user traffic in its data field), the PPP protocol number ranges between x0000 and x3FFF. The value is the same as the NCP value less x8000.

ADDRESS MANAGEMENT AND ASSIGNMENT OPERATIONS

One of the greatest benefits of using a dial-in protocol (such as PPP) is the ability to manage network addresses more efficiently. Instead of using static addresses, an address can be assigned only when a user is logged on to the network. After the user logs off, the address is placed back into an address pool, to be used by someone else.

Most routers support dynamic address assignment with a PPP NCP and the Network Address Translation (NAT) protocol, published in RFC 1631.[1] Before we examine the NCPs, we will take a look at address pools, dynamic address assignment, and the NAT.

The Network Address Translation (NAT) allows an organization to use private, nonregistered IP addresses (nonglobally routable addresses) within its own routing domain. If traffic is to be sent out of this domain, NAT translates these addresses to globally routable addresses. The reverse process occurs at the NAT router for traffic received by the domain. NAT thus allows an organization to use its own private addresses. It also supports a process called the TCP load distribution feature that allows the mapping of a single global address to multiple nonglobal addresses. This feature is used to conserve addresses and is explained shortly. NAT is described in RFC 1631, and examples used in this discussion are sourced from this RFC and several Cisco manuals.

Figure 4–1 is used to introduce the basic concepts of NAT. First, a couple of definitions are in order. An *inside local IP address* is a nonglobal address that is assigned to a host. This host resides on an inside network—one that uses nonglobal addresses. An *inside global IP address* is a global address and represents the inside address to the outside networks (global addressing networks). Router A in this figure houses a NAT table that correlates these addresses.

The bottom part of Figure 4–1 shows how NAT is used to map addresses between the inside and outside networks. In event 1, host B sends an IP datagram to host D, through router A. Router A checks the address in the datagram and knows that source address (SA) 176.16.1.1 is an inside address. If an entry in the NAT table does not exist, the router dynamically selects an available global address from a pool of addresses, and creates an entry in the table. In event 2, the router replaces the inside SA with the corresponding outside SA, and forwards the datagram.

---

[1]Cisco's product to provide this service is called Easy IP.

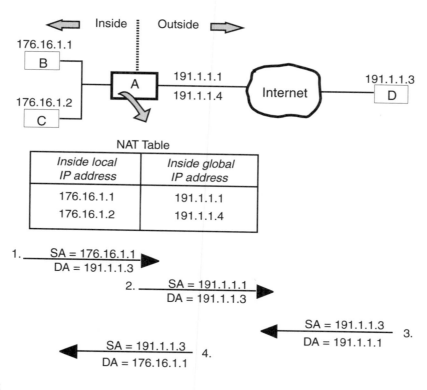

Figure 4–1   Network Address Translation (NAT)

In event 3, host D replies, and uses its SA of 191.1.1.3, and the NAT global address for the destination address (DA) of 191.1.1.1. This datagram is received by router A, which performs the mapping of the global DA of 191.1.1.1 to the inside DA of 176.16.1.1, depicted as event 4 in Figure 4–1.

NAT is a straightforward configuration; essentially the local IP and global IP addresses are entered into the table during the configuration, along with the inside and outside interfaces on the router.

NAT allows the reuse of inside global addresses by mapping one of these addresses to more than one local address. This operation is called *overloading an inside global address*. The ability to maintain unambiguous identification of all user sessions is through the inside local address, the inside global address, plus the port numbers that are carried in the TCP or UDP segment header.

NAT defines another address; it is called the *outside global IP address*, which is a conventional IP address assigned to a host on the globally addressable outside network.

Figure 4–2 shows how this part of NAT works. In event 1, host B sends a datagram to host D, through router A. The figure shows the

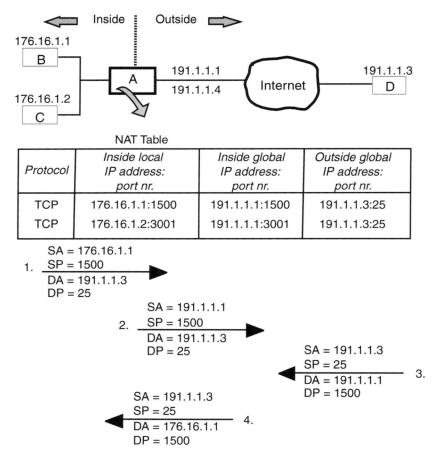

Figure 4–2   Overloading inside global addresses

source address (SA), source port (SP), destination address (DA), and destination port (DP). The router intercepts the datagram, and it performs either static or dynamic translation of the inside local IP address (176.16.1.1) to a shared inside global IP address (191.1.1.1).

In event 2, the router forwards the datagram toward the destination host D. In event 3, host D replies. The host simply exchanges the destination address and port number with the source address and port number.

Router A receives this datagram, and looks at the NAT table to determine what it is to do. It uses the socket pair shown in event 3 as a key to the table.

In event 4, the translation is made back to host B's inside local IP address and the datagram is delivered to host B in the inside network.

The same operation can be performed for host C, using the second entry in the NAT table, which is host C's routing table entry.

The configuration at the router entails the allocation of a pool of global addresses as needed, and then correlating them with the inside addresses and the associated input and output interfaces.

THE INTERNET PROTOCOL CONTROL PROTOCOL (IPCP)

RFC 1332 defines the PPP Internet Protocol Control Protocol (IPCP). It is a short and straightforward specification and concerns itself with only three options, one of which is deprecated. Its protocol number is x8021, and the corresponding network protocol number is x0021.

IPCP operates like other NCPs, and requires that the link is configured and tested before it executes. It uses the same packet exchange mechanism as LCP, described in Chapter 3. IPCP packets may not be exchanged until PPP has reached the Network-Layer Protocol phase. IPCP packets received before this phase is reached are silently discarded.

The IPCP is exactly the same as the LCP with the following exceptions (and see Box 4–1 for a summary of these rules):

- Exactly one IPCP packet is encapsulated in the Information field of PPP Data-Link Layer frames where the protocol field indicates type x8021 (IPCP).
- Only Codes 1 through 7 (Configure-Request, Configure-ACK, Configure-NAK, Configure-Reject, Terminate-Request, Terminate-ACK, and Code-Reject) are used. Other Codes result in Code-Rejects.

Box 4–1   RFC 1332: Summary of PPP Internet Protocol Control Protocol (IPCP)

- Used to set up, negotiate, and encapsulate IP
- One IPCP packet is encapsulated in PPP Protocol field = x8021 (IP Control Protocol)
- One IP packet is encapsulated in PPP frames Protocol field = x0021 (Internet Protocol)
- Two options cited in RFC 1332:
    Compression
    IP address assignments

- One IP packet is encapsulated in the Information field of PPP frames where the Protocol field indicates type x0021 (Internet Protocol).
- The maximum length of an IP packet transmitted over a PPP link is the same as the maximum length of the Information field of a PPP data link layer frame. Larger IP datagrams must be fragmented as necessary.

Configuration Options

The IPCP Configuration Options allow negotiation of Internet Protocol parameters. Current values are assigned as follows:

IP-Addresses (option code 01): This option, described in RFC 1171, is deprecated. It is replaced by the IP-Address option described below.

IP-Compression-Protocol (option code 02): Compression is a common operation invoked to reduce the number of bytes carried across a link. For this option, the data field contains the identifier of the compression protocol and specific information about the compression protocol. Compression operations are described in RFC 1332. Van Jacobson Compressed TCP/IP is the protocol cited in this RFC. It is used to compress the TCP and IP headers.

IP-Address (option code 03): This option sets up an IP address on the user end of the link (usually). If it is not used, no addresses are assigned. It allows the sender of the Configure-Req packet to state which IP address is desired, or to request that the peer provide the information. The peer provides this information by NAKing the option, and returning a valid IP address. A common use of this option is when a customer dials in to an ISP, and the ISP assigns the customer an address from the ISP's pool of addresses.

Option 03 need not be used. It is certainly possible to use preconfigured addresses and assign them manually. The advantage of this option is that servers can be assigned to remote locations and easily identified. In addition, if the addresses are part of an enterprise's network, they are transparent to outsiders (by using address masking). However, manual administration of addresses is a difficult task and subject to errors. Static addresses are just that, static, and a device uses the address even when it is off-line. All-in-all, it makes more sense to use this PPP option.

Most routers today contain software that perform these services. Obviously the router must be configured to support dynamic address assignment, and a pool of addresses must be set up, as well as a number of other configuration parameters. After the configuration is completed, address assignment is automatic.

As a quick summary of IPCP and NAT, the joint use of these protocols:

(a) Reduces costs by reusing purchased addresses.

(b) Conserves the IP address space.

(c) Eases the tasks of address management.

(d) Provides a security screen in front of the customer's IP addresses.

Mobile-IPv4 (option code 89): This option is becoming more important as mobile nodes acquire more data communications capabilities. Mobile IP allows a mobile node to retain its assigned home ("permanent") address when it moves to another network (subnet).

Without the use of Mobile IP, a mobile station node would have to change its IP address whenever it moves to a new network (that is, whenever it changes its point of attachment). Additionally, without the use of Mobile IP, routes specific to the host would have to be propagated into the networks that are concerned with supporting this host. Obviously, these two operations are not efficient and would create tremendous housekeeping problems for the network. In addition, due to the nature in which IP addresses are used to identify higher-layer connections (sockets to the applications themselves), it becomes an impossible task to maintain this relationship if the IP address changes.

The value in the option field is an IP address sent by a mobile node back to its home agent (a router that receives all the mobile node's traffic from other nodes). The mobile node requests the home agent to forward the mobile node's traffic on to the mobile node.

Option 89 has some of features of the Mobile IP specification dealing with mobile-node registrations. It is unlikely both procedures (option 89 and the Mobile IP) are implemented in a mobile system because they have some overlapping functions.

Other Options: There are other ICMP options which can be used in IPCP. They deal with the Domain Name Service (DNS) and the NETBIOS name server (NBNS). They have not seen extensive use. RFC 1877 describes these options if you wish more information on them.

THE INTERNET PROTOCOL VERSION 6 CONTROL PROTOCOL (IPv6CP)

With the increased interest in IPv6 and the increasing use of PPP, it is probable (eventually) that IPv6 will run over PPP. This section describes these operations. A more thorough explanation is available in RFC 2023, and IPv6 is described in RFC 1883.

Before any IPv6 packets are transmitted, PPP must reach the Network-Layer Protocol phase, and the IPv6CP must reach the Opened state. One IPv6 packet is encapsulated in the information field of the PPP frame [see Figure 4–3(a)]. The protocol field indicates type x0057 (IPv6). The maximum length of an IPv6 packet transmitted over a PPP link is the same as the maximum length of the information field of a PPP frame.

The IPv6CP is responsible for configuring, enabling, and disabling the IPv6 protocol modules on both ends of the link. IPv6CP uses the same packet-exchange mechanism as the Link Control Protocol (LCP). IPv6CP datagrams are not exchanged until PPP reaches the Network-Layer Protocol phase. IPv6CP packets received before this phase is reached are silently discarded. The IPv6CP is the same as the LCP with the following exceptions.

One IPv6CP packet is encapsulated in the Information field of PPP frames when the Protocol field indicates type x8057 (IPv6CP [see Figure 4–3(b)]. Codes 1 through 7 are used. Other Codes are rejected. The IPv6CP has a distinct set of Configuration Options, which are explained below.

The IPv6CP Configuration Options allow negotiation of several IPv6 parameters. IPv6CP uses the same Configuration Option format defined for LCP, with a separate set of options. Up-to-date values of the IPv6CP

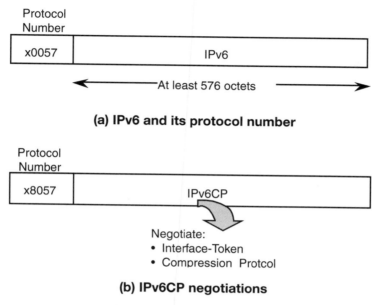

(a) IPv6 and its protocol number

(b) IPv6CP negotiations

Figure 4–3   IPv6 and PPP

Option Type field are specified in the most recent "Assigned Numbers" RFC 1700. Current values are assigned for:

(a) Interface Token

(b) IPv6-Compression-Protocol

The interface-token Configuration Option provides a way to negotiate a unique 32-bit interface token to be used for the address auto-configuration at the local end of the link. The interface token is unique within the PPP link[2]; upon completion of the negotiation different interface-token values are to be selected for the ends of the PPP link.

The IPv6 Configuration Option supports the negotiation of the use of a specific IPv6 packet compression protocol. The IPv6-Compression-Protocol Configuration Option is used to indicate the ability to receive compressed datagrams. Each end of the link requests this option if bidirectional compression is used.

---

[2]RFC 2023 provides several suggestions on obtaining a unique value for the interface token.

OTHER NETWORK PROTOCOLS

The emphasis thus far in the chapter has been IP. It is the prevalent L_3 protocol in the industry, and will continue to gain market share. However, several other L_3 protocols are still used in the industry, and some are widely used. This part of the chapter examines the NCP associated with each. A table is provided with each explanation that summarizes the options for each NCP.

OPEN SYSTEMS INTERCONNECTION NCP (OSINLCP)

The OSI Connectionless-Layer Network Protocol (CLNP) is used in some systems in place of IP. It is similar in function to IP, but has more capabilities. The NCP is OSINLCP and is identified with protocol control number x8023, and the protocol itself is identifed with protocol number x0023.

Interestingly, the first octet of the CLNP data is yet another encapsulation header, named the network-level protocol identifier (NLPID). This value indicates which OSI protocol is in the CLNP data field. Originally, NLPID contained only ISO- or ITU-T-sanctioned protocols, thus ignoring a rather prevalent protocol, IP. Later, the ISO 9577 standard was amended to allow the identification of other protocols. For Internet traffic, it reserves hex values of x0080 for the Subnetwork Access Protocol (SNAP) and x00CC for IP.

Some systems have a rather convoluted way of identifying the nature of the payload in the packet. For example, the PPP protocol ID is set to x0023 to indicate CLNP traffic. Next, the CLNP NLPID is set to x0080 to indicate a SNAP header follows next. Then the SNAP header also has an encapsulation identifier that finally identifies the payload! This is the approach taken by Frame Relay to identify its payload when it is carrying PPP encapsulated traffic.

The OSINLCP RFC and option is summarized in Table 4–1. The only option, align with PPP I field, is used for aligning the CLNP bytes within the PPP I field, and providing padding, if necessary.

System Network Architecture (SNA) NCP (SNACP)

IBM's SNA is a widely used proprietary protocol stack used between IBM mainframe computers, terminal controllers and terminals (see Table 4–2). The SNACP has no options and is assigned two protocol numbers: (a)

Table 4–1   The OSINLCP

Name	Sponsor	RFC(s)	Options
OSILNCP	ISO & ITU-T	1377	01 Align with PPP I field

SNA with Advanced Peer-to-Peer Networking High-Performance Routing (APPN-HPR), and (b) SNA over LLC 802.2. For (a), x804D is the control protocol ID, and x004D is the network protocol number. For (b), x804B is the control protocol ID, and x004B is the network protocol number.

Since no negotiations take place, the initial Configure-Request packet contains no additional parameters, nor does the returning Configure-ACK or Protocol-Reject packet.

NetBIOS Frames NCP (NBFCP)

NetBIOS is an IBM protocol that has been around for many years and was implemented to support PC communications. It contains both layer-3 and layer-4 services. The control protocol is x803F, and the network protocol is x003F. Table 4–3 summarizes the options for NetBIOS. Options 01, 02, and 04 are used to exchange identifiers, software version numbers, and L_2 MAC addresses, if necessary. Option 03 places a limit on the number of multicast messages that a peer can send out.

Internetwork Packet Exchange NCP (IPXCP)

The Internetwork Packet Exchange Protocol (IPX) has seen extensive use in the industry, due to Novell using it as part of its LAN product line. It is derived from the work of Xerox and XNS. IPXCP is assigned protocol control number x802B, and the corresponding IPX is assigned protocol number x002B.

Six options are defined for IPXCP, and are summarized in Table 4–4. Option 01 is used to assign a network address to the link. It is not neces-

Table 4–2   The SNACP

Name	Sponsor	RFC(s)	Options
SNACP	IBM	2043	None

Table 4–3   The NBFCP

Name	Sponsor	RFC(s)	Options
NBFCP	IBM	2097	01 Name-Projection: Exchange network IDs 02 Peer-Information: Exchange version numbers of software 03 Multicast-Filtering: Limits number of multicasts 04 IEEE-MAC-Address-Required: Transmits MAC address

sary to have two network addresses on a point-to-point link, and this option assigns only one network number. Option 02 assigns two L_2 addresses (which can be a MAC address or another address, unique to the system), one on each end of the link. Option 03 negotiates the use of header compression (either the Telebit compression or the Shiva compression algorithms). Option 04 establishes the routing protocol that is to be used during the session, such as the Routing Information Protocol (RIP) or Novell's routing protocols. Option 05 allows the peers to exchange a name with each other; for example, a domain name of a server. Finally, option 06 is used to hasten the completion of the negotiations by sending a Configure-Request packet to inform the peer that the negotiation process is over.

Bridge NCP (BCP)

In situations where a bridge is employed between two LANs (full bridge) or between a LAN and a point-to-point link (half-bridge), the

Table 4–4   The IPXCP

Name	Sponsor	RFC(s)	Options
PXCP	Novell	1552 1634	01 IPX-Network-Number: Assigns address to the link 02 IPX-Node-Number: Assigns L_2 address to the link 03 IPX-Compression: Negotiates header compression 04 IPX-Routing-Protocol: Negotiates routing protocol 05 IPX-Router-Name: Provides a name to the peer 06 IPX-Configuration-Complete: Completes negotiations

bridge NCP can be used to negotiate several options. Alternately, a router interface can be configured for PPP half-bridging. This feature uses protocol number x0031 and control number x8031.

Figure 4–4 shows a configuration for a half-bridge. The router interface acts as a node on the Ethernet subnetwork attached to the bridge and has an IP address on the same Ethernet subnet as the bridge.

The router is configured for PPP half-bridging with a few simple crafting commands. One command sets up the network address with the specific PPP link interface. Another command defines which network protocols will be supported on the interface (IP, IPX, AppleTalk, etc.). Another command must be entered before PPP can operate; it is usually called an enable command. Thereafter, PPP is used to set up the session between the router and the bridge.

As stated earlier, the PPP bridging operation supports the half-bridge or the full-bridge. In the half-bridge operation, the bridge and the router in Figure 4–4 interwork as if they belong to the same subnet and are part of one "virtual" bridge. In this situation, PPP is transparent to the bridge-spanning tree operations (explained shortly). In the full-bridge operation, the PPP link in Figure 4–4 is included in the spanning tree operations.

BCP includes seven options that are summarized in Table 4–5. Option 01 is used to inform the peer that a half-bridge operation is in place at the interface. During this handshake, the peers exchange information on the LAN segment number, and the bridge ID (defined in IEEE 802.1d specifications).

Option 02 is used to inform the peer that a full-bridge operation is in place at the interface. The information exchanged is the same as in op-

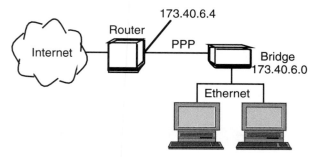

Figure 4–4 PPP half-bridging or full-bridging

Table 4–5   The BCP

Name	Sponsor	RFC(s)	Options
BCP	IETF	1638	01 Bridge Identification: Use half-bridge operation
			02 Line Identification: Use full-bridge operation
			03 MAC Support: Defines type of MAC LAN on the interface
			04 Tinygram Compression: Negotiate compression
			05 LAN Identification: Check LAN ID for forwarding choice
			06 MAC address: Set up (announce) local MAC address
			07 Spanning Tree Protocol (STP): Negotiate specific STP

tion 01. Notice that either option 01 or 02 are set up between the peers; they are not set up simultaneously.

Option 03 sets up the specific MAC LAN protocol to be executed. The data field in this packet can identify various LANs such as Ethernet, token bus, token ring, FDDI, etc.

Option 04 sets up or disables compression. This operation is not the same as the header compression operations discussed earlier in this chapter. In numerous operations in an internet, the size of the packet (protocol data unit, or PDU) sent by a user application may be small, perhaps only about 40 or so bytes. Ethernet requires at least 64 bytes in a PDU. So, this option allows the padding bytes that are inserted at the sender to meet Ethernet requirements to be stripped away for link transmission and then be reconstructed by the peer.

Option 05 is used to inform the peer that it must examine the LAN ID field to divide the incoming traffic based on this identifier, and distribute the traffic accordingly. If this option is disabled, a packet that has the LAN ID field in it will not be processed.

Option 06 is used to assign a MAC address or to request the assignment of a MAC address. Its use is limited to Ethernet LANs and for bridges. For more details, see RFC 1638.

Option 07 is used to set up a specific implementation of a spanning tree protocol.

AppleTalk NCP (ATCP)

AppleTalk is a proprietary protocol that runs on Apple computers. It has many similarities to the OSI protocol stack, and its lower layers resemble other conventional protocols. The AppleTalk Control Protocol is x8029, and the network protocol is x0029.

Table 4–6   The ATCP

Name	Sponsor	RFC(s)	Options
ATCP	Apple	1378	01 AppleTalk Address: Exchange network & node number
			02 Routing Protocol: Set up L_3 routing protocol
			03 Suppress Broadcast: Selective filtering of broadcasts
			04 Compression: Implement header compression
			05 Reserved
			06 Server Information: Identifies type of server to a peer
			07 Zone Information: Provides zone name to a node
			08 Default Router Address: Identified default router

Table 4–6 lists the eight options provided in ATCP. Most of them are self-explanatory, but a few comments are in order. Options 01 and 08 perform the same functions. The difference is that option 08 is used to inform a node that a specific router (among more than one router) should be used for this node to forward traffic. Option 02 is used because AppleTalk supports more than one L_3 routing protocol.

Xerox Network Systems Internet Datagram NCP (XNSCP)

The Xerox Network Systems (XNS) network protocol is x0025, and its control protocol is x8025. It has no configuration options. I make no further mention of XNS because it is being phased out of the industry. But I would like to take a brief digression and give a salute to Xerox and the Xerox Palo Alto Research Center (PARC). XNS and other Xerox-inspired technologies have provided the data communications industry with farsighted and practical tools. Their legacy is found in IP, IPX, AppleTalk, and of course, the Macintosh and Windows Graphical User Interface (GUI).

Banyan Vines NCP (BVCP)

The Banyan Vines protocol number is x0035, and the control protocol number is x8035. Table 4–7 lists the four options associated with Vines. Option 01 is used to determine how often routing updates are sent by a node. Option 02 is used to invoke the user of Vines Fragmentation Protocol (FRP). Option 03 suppresses routing updates on a link, for example a PPP link (which is a static route). Option 04 suppresses broad-

Table 4–7   The BVCP

Name	Sponsor	RFC(s)	Options
BVCP	Banyan	1763	01 Determines behavior of routing updates
			02 Configures Vines fragmentation protocol
			03 Suppresses routing updates
			04 Supresses broadcast messages

cast messages on a LAN with the exception of broadcast for address mapping protocols (ARP) and routing protocols.

DECnet Phase IV NCP (DNCP)

DECnet Phase IV over PPP is defined in RFC 1762. The network protocol number is x0027, and the network control protocol number is x8027. It has no options and uses only the PPP Configure-Request and Configure-ACK messages. PPP encapsulates DECnet IV routing packets only, and not the other DECnet IV control packets (LAT, etc.).

SUMMARY

After the LCP has completed its operation, an NCP is invoked. The main task of the NCP is to configure (negotiate) an L_3 protocol between the PPP peers. Some L_2 operations can also be negotiated if LAN bridges are part of the configuration.

The Internet Protocol Control Protocol (IPCP) is the most widely NCP because it is used for setting up IP and negotiating header compression and the assignment of an IP address to the client. The Network Address Translation (NAT) Protocol is a prevalent protocol for managing the IP addresses.

5

PPP Security Operations

This chapter introduces the Internet security services and explains how several protocols are used in conjunction with PPP by a client to obtain these services. The focus is on four protocols: (a) the Password Authentication Protocol (PAP), (b) the Challenge-Handshake Authentication Protocol (CHAP), (c) the Remote Authentication Dial-In User Service (RADIUS), and (d) the IP Security Protocol (IPSec).

The subject of Internet security warrants a separate book, and one is being written for this series. Our goal in this chapter is to highlight the subject in relation to PPP.

WHAT IS INTERNET SECURITY?

When the term Internet security is mentioned to some people, and they are asked what it means, a common response is, "It means encrypting the traffic that flows through the Internet." Yes, but it means more than just encrypting traffic. Internet security means the use of encryption to achieve three major goals:

- *Privacy/Secrecy*: The assurance that an Internet user's traffic is not examined by nonauthorized parties. In so many words, it is an assurance that no one "reads your mail." The term *confidentiality* is also used to describe this service.

- *Authentication*: The assurance that the traffic you receive (e-mail, files, Web pages, etc.) is sent by the legitimate party or parties. For example, if you receive a legal document from your attorney through the Internet, you are confident that your attorney sent it—not someone else.
- *Integrity*: The assurance that the traffic you receive has not been modified after it was sent by the proper party. This service includes anti-replay defenses; that is, operations that prevent someone from reinjecting previously authenticated packets into a traffic stream.

These three security services need not be invoked for each piece of traffic sent through an internet. For example, a user (say, Ted) may not care if someone reads Ted's mail; Ted may only care that the receiver (say Carol) has confidence that the mail indeed came from Ted. Of course, Carol also cares about the authenticity of Ted. In this example, Ted and Carol are concerned with authentication, but not privacy.

The manner in which an organization or person decides on the combinations of these security services is the subject of later discussions. Now, let us concentrate on the procedures used by PPP to obtain security services. But first, a word or two for the newcomer about encryption keys.

ENCRYPTION KEYS

An encryption key is a value that is used with an encryption algorithm to change cleartext (readable text) to ciphertext (not readable text). The ciphertext is created at the sending user's site and relayed to the receiving user's site, where the process is reversed. A decryption key is used with the decryption algorithm to change the ciphertext back to the original cleartext.

This process assumes that the two parties share a key, and no one else has access to it, else a third party could decipher the encrypted traffic. Thus, this key is called a secret key, because it is known only by the sending and receiving parties.

Private and Public Keys

Two forms of encryption are used in the industry. One is called the private key operation, which entails the use of one key (the private key) shared between the two parties. The other form is called the public key operation, which entails the use of two keys. One key is called the public key, and the other key is called the private key.

Public keys have been used in private and public networks for a number of years for the encryption of data. The public key concept rests on the idea of calculating two keys from one function. As just mentioned, one key is called the public key and the other key is called the private key. They are so-named because the public key can be disseminated to a body-at-large, whereas the private key is not disseminated.

The creator of the private key keeps this key in a secure manner. If this key is disseminated, it is done by first encrypting it for transmission to the receiver. Notwithstanding, the idea of the public key is to keep the private key close-to-the-vest, and not reveal its contents to anyone but the creator(s).

Public keys can be used for encryption and authentication. In Figure 5–1, the sender uses the receiver's public key to encrypt the clear text of a message into the ciphered message. The process is reversed at the receiver, where the receiver uses the private key to decrypt the ciphered message into the clear text. This encryption operation thus provides privacy/security of the user's traffic.

In addition to the use of public keys for encryption, they are widely used for authentication procedures, as shown in Figure 5–2. In this example, the sender uses the sender's private key to encrypt a known value into the *Digital Signature*. The purpose of the Digital Signature is to validate the authenticity of the sender. Consequently, through other measures, the sender has sent to the receiver the sender's public key. This key is applied

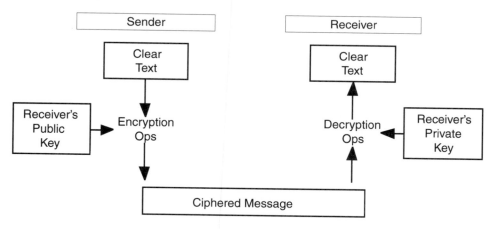

Figure 5–1   Encryption for confidentiality

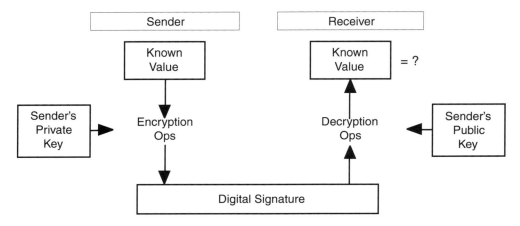

Figure 5–2   Encryption for authentication

(with an algorithm) to the incoming Digital Signature. If the resulting decryption operations result in the computation of the known value that was initially instantiated by the sender, then the sender is considered to be the legitimate sender (that is, the sender is authentic).

In summary, if the computed known value at the receiver is equal to the expected value, then the sender has been authenticated. If the computation is not equal, then the sender is not authentic or an error has occurred in the processing. Whatever the case may be, the sender is not allowed any further privileges at the receiver's system.

Distribution of Keys

Since the communicating parties are not co-located, there must be some means of exchanging keys with each other. One might just put them in express mail, but that method is not very secure. Anyway, there are a number of methods to disseminate keys, and for the remainder of this chapter, we assume the PPP peers have used these methods to obtain each other's secret key. For more information on this aspect of security, I refer you to the security text in this series.

THE PASSWORD AUTHENTICATION PROTOCOL (PAP)

RFC 1334 defines PPP authentication procedures for two authentication protocols: (a) the Password Authentication Protocol (PAP), and (b) the Challenge-Handshake Authentication Protocol (CHAP). CHAP is now published in a more recent specification, RFC 1994 (which does not include PAP). This discussion concentrates on PAP, while CHAP is discussed next.

PAP is a simple procedure for a peer (usually a host, or router) to establish its identity by using a two-way handshake. This operation is performed upon initial link establishment. Once the Link Establishment phase is complete, an ID/Password pair is repeatedly sent by the peer to the authenticator (the node responsible for verifying the operation) until authentication is acknowledged or the connection is terminated.

PAP is not intended to be a strong authentication procedure, and all passwords and IDs are sent across the link in the clear. The nodes have no protection against monitoring or security attacks.

Then why use it? RFC 1334 states that it is most appropriately used where a plaintext password must be available to simulate a login at a remote host. In such use, this method provides a similar level of security to the conventional user login at the remote host. Nonetheless, PAP is not used much in the Internet.

Figure 5–3 shows the format of the PPP protocol data unit for PAP. The PPP protocol field is set to xC023 for PAP. The code field identifies one of three PPP packets: (a) the Authenticate-Request, (b) the Authenticate-ACK, and (c) the Authenticate-NAK. The ID and Length fields are coded in accordance with conventional rules discussed earlier. The Data field is coded with a Peer-id and Password in the Authenticate-Request packet, and a message in the ACK or ACK packets.

Here is a summary of the key aspects of PAP. First, the Authenticate-Request packet is used to begin the PAP operations. The link peer must send the Authenticate-Request packet during the PPP Authentication phase. The Authenticate-Request packet is repeated until a valid reply packet is received, or an optional retry counter expires.

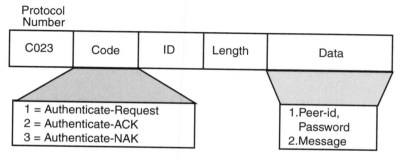

Figure 5–3   Password Authentication Protocol (PAP)

The authenticator expects the peer to send an Authenticate-Request packet. Upon reception of an Authenticate-Request packet, some type of Authenticate reply is returned. However, authentication begins with the authenticatee, and not the authenticator.

If the Peer-ID/Password pair received in an Authenticate-Request is both recognizable and acceptable, then the authenticator sends an Authenticate-ACK. Otherwise, it sends an Authenticate-NAK. In this case, this party is not authenticated, and L_3 packets cannot be exchanged. The recipient of the NAK must clear the link.

THE CHALLENGE-HANDSHAKE AUTHENTICATION PROTOCOL (CHAP)

The Challenge-Handshake Authentication Protocol is published in RFC 1994 [SIMP96].[1] Like PAP, it is designed to operate over PPP dial-up links between a host and another node, such as a NAS. In this part of our analysis, we take a look at the major attributes of CHAP.

CHAP is a strong authentication protocol. It uses secret keys between the peers. However, RFC 1994 discusses an important caveat:

> CHAP requires that the secret be available in plaintext form. Irreversibly encrypted password databases commonly available cannot be used.
>
> It is not as useful for large installations, since every possible secret is maintained at both ends of the link.
>
> Implementation Note: To avoid sending the secret over other links in the network, it is recommended that the challenge and response values be examined at a central server, rather than each network access server. Otherwise, the secret SHOULD be sent to such servers in a reversably encrypted form. Either case requires a trusted relationship, which is outside the scope of this specification.

CHAP periodically verifies the identity of the peer using a three-way handshake during the initial link establishment. Thereafter, CHAP can be invoked at any time.

After the completion of the PPP Link Establishment phase, the authenticator sends a challenge message to its peer (a random number). This peer must then calculate a one-way hash function and send this information to the authenticator. This response depends on the challenge

---

[1][SIMP96] Simpson, W. "PPP Challenge Handshake Authentication Protocol (CHAP)", RFC 1994, August, 1996.

and a secret key. The one-way hash function must be one in which it is computationally not feasible to derive the secret key from the known challenge and response values.

The authenticator verifies the hash value with its complementary calculation and responds with an ACK if the values match. Otherwise, the connection is terminated. Unlike PAP, the process is controlled by the authenticator and not the authenticatee.

CHAP uses an incrementally changing identifier and a variable challenge value. The use of repeated challenges is intended to limit the time of exposure to any single attack. The authenticator is in control of the frequency and timing of the challenges. As stated earlier, the authentication method depends upon a "secret" known only to the authenticator and that peer. The secret is not sent over the link.

Authentication is one-way, but PPP's two-way behavior allows CHAP to actually operate in a two-way fashion.

CHAP can be used to authenticate different systems, so name fields are used as an index to locate the proper secret in a table of secrets. This concept also makes it possible to support more than one name/secret pair per system, and to change the secret in use at any time during the session.

Figure 5–4 shows the packet exchanged between the two parties involved in a CHAP authentication operation.

The CHAP Packets

An authentication protocol can be negotiated, during the LCP negotiation phase. RFC 1661 defines LCP type = 3 (the configuration option) in the LCP type field to identify an authentication protocol. Figure 5–5

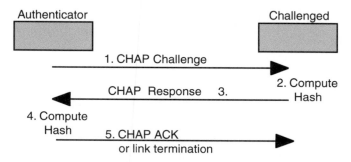

Figure 5–4   Challenge-Handshake Authentication Protocol (CHAP)

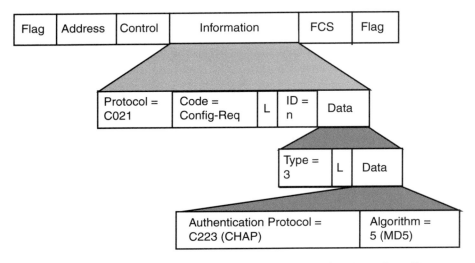

Figure 5–5   The LCP configure-request packet to set up the use of CHAP

shows the format and contents of the LCP packet used to begin the negotiation for the use of CHAP on the PPP link.

Most of the fields in this packet have been described in Chapter 3. Let's review some of these fields and introduce the others. The L fields are length fields, explained earlier. The PPP protocol is xC021 to identify LCP. The code field is set to identify an LCP Configure-Request packet (code = 1, as defined in RFC 1661). The length (L) and ID fields are filled in as described in Chapter 3. The data field contains the type field, which is set to 3. In accordance with RFC 1661, the type value of 3 signifies that the peer wishes to negotiate the use of an authentication protocol. The data fields for type 3 indicate the specific authentication protocol the peer wishes to use, and the security algorithm for the authentication; in this example, the Message Digest 5 algorithm. These two fields are set to xC223 and 5, respectively, in accordance with RFC 1994.

After the LCP has negotiated the use of CHAP, the authentication takes place by the exchange of the CHAP packets, and the hash functions explained earlier in this chapter. The CHAP packets used for the authentication are: (a) Challenge, (b) Response, (c) Success, (d) Failure. They are coded in two formats, shown in Figure 5–6. The overall structure of the PPP packet is described earlier. For this discussion, the identifier is changed each time a Challenge is sent, and this field is copied into the associated Response.

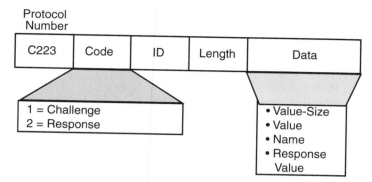

(a) Challenge/Response message

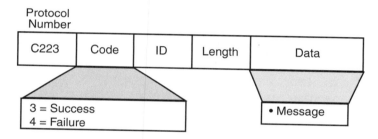

(b) Success/Failure message

Figure 5–6   CHAP messages

As shown in the data field in Figure 5–6 (a), the Value-Size field indicates the size of the Value field. The Value field in the Challenge message is the Challenge value. RFC 1994 states that each Challenge value should be unique, since repetition of a Challenge value in conjunction with the same secret would permit an attacker to reply with a previously intercepted response. Furthermore, each value should be as random and unpredictable as possible and must be changed with each Challenge.

The Response packet is the result of the hash calculation. The response is calculated over a stream of concatenated octets consisting of the Identifier, followed by the secret, followed by the Challenge Value. The length of the Response Value depends on the hash algorithm (for example, it is 128 bits for MD 5, which is the prevalent algorithm used in dial-up authentication). As expected, the one-way hash algorithm is chosen such that it is computationally infeasible to determine the secret from the known challenge and response values.

The Name field is used to identify the system that transmits the CHAP message. No limitation is placed on how this field is coded.

In Figure 5–6(b), a Success is sent back to the peer if the Value received is the same as the expected value. Otherwise, a Failure is returned. In the latter case, the link should be terminated. For the Success and Failure messages, the Message field is implementation-specific.

RADIUS

In a large organization, the security operations are a significant chore and require the commitment of many financial and personnel resources. One of the ongoing concerns of the network administrator is the possible compromise of the organization's resources due to the dispersal of security measures throughout the enterprise, resulting in a fragmented approach. To compound matters, employees, contractors, and customers need access to information, and these individuals may dial in to the organization's computers from practically anywhere. Authentication of these diverse sources must be accomplished in accordance with the organization's security policy. But how? Should there be an authentication system (a server) at each of the organization's sites? If so, how are these servers managed, how are their activities coordinated? How are the keys disseminated? Should the organization deploy one centralized server to reduce the coordination efforts?

To aid an organization in establishing an integrated approach to security management, the Internet Network Working Group has published RFC 2138, the Remote Authentication Dial-In User Service (RADIUS). This specification defines the procedures to implement an authentication server, containing a central database that identifies the dial-in users, and the associated information to authenticate the users.

RADIUS also permits the server to consult with other servers, some may be RADIUS-based, and some may not. With this approach, the RADIUS server acts as proxy to the other server. The specification also details how the user's specific operations can be supported, such as PPP, rlogin, telnet, etc.

Example of RADIUS Configuration

Figure 5–7 shows the configuration for RADIUS, which is built on a client/server model. The end user communicates with a Network Access Server (NAS) through a dial-up link. In turn, the NAS is the client to the

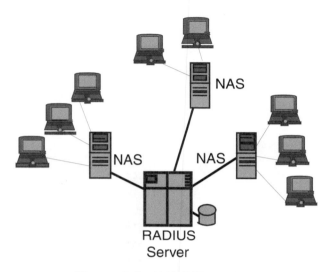

Figure 5–7   RADIUS configuration

RADIUS server. The NAS and RADIUS server communicate with each other through a network, or a point-to-point link. As mentioned earlier, the RADIUS server may communicate with other servers, some may operate the RADIUS protocol, and some may not. Also, the idea is to have a central repository for the authentication information, shown in this figure as the database icon.

The user is required to present authentication information to the NAS (called the client hereafter), such as a user name and a password, or a PPP authentication packet. The client may then access RADIUS. If so, the client creates a RADIUS Access Request packet and sends the packet to the RADIUS node (called the server hereafter). This message contains information about the user, called Attributes. The Attributes are defined by the RADIUS system manager, and therefore can vary. Examples of Attributes are the user's password, ID, destination port, client ID, etc. If sensitive information is contained in the Attributes field, it must be protected by the Message Digest Algorithm MD5, or another security algorithm.

The RADIUS Packet Exchange

Figure 5–8 shows a typical packet exchange for a RADIUS-based authentication. The operation begins with the client entering into a PPP LCP logon procedure with the user (event 1). This information is used by the client to communicate with the RADIUS server, shown in events 2

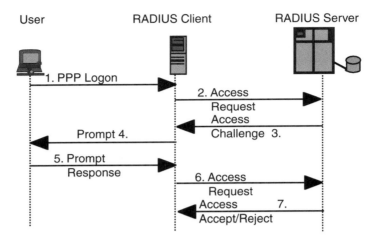

Figure 5–8   RADIUS operation

and 3. The RADIUS client issues an Access-Request packet which must include a shared secret with the RADIUS server. Otherwise, the Access-Request packet is silently discarded (nothing happens—no further processing). If the initial check is satisfactory, the server consults a database to authenticate the user. The database contains the information to validate the user, that is, a list of validation requirements.

If the authentication conditions are met, the server issues a challenge to the user in the form of an Access Challenge packet. The client may relay this information to the user in the form of a prompt, and wait for a reply (events 4 and 5). These events take place with PPP, CHAP, etc.

Whatever the scenario may be between the user and the client, the client must resubmit the Access Request packet, shown as event 6 in the figure. This packet contains several fields; the salient one for this example is an encrypted response to the challenge. The user is "challenged" by being presented with a random number, and tasked with encrypting it, and sending back the result of the encryption. The server receives and examines this packet. If all conditions are satisfied, the server returns an Access Accept packet to the client, shown as event 7.

However, the RADIUS protocol goes much further than the support of authentication operations. The Access Accept packet contains configuration information, such as PPP, login user, etc. The idea is to use the RADIUS node to give the client all the information needed to support the user session with the network. As examples, the configuration information can be an IP address for the session, compression services, and the maximum transmission unit size (MTU).

Events 4 and 5 may occur earlier in this example. For example, they may take place just after event 1. I place them in this example, as occurring after the RADIUS client and RADIUS server have performed their handshake.

Let us assume that the RADIUS client is an NAS and supports PAP and CHAP. The NAS user sends the PAP ID and password in the Access Request message in the User-Name and User-Password fields of the message. If CHAP is used, the NAS node generates a challenge and sends it to the user. In accordance with CHAP conventions, the user responds with the CHAP ID and CHAP user name. The NAS node then sends to the RADIUS server the Access Request packet, containing the CHAP user name, as well as the CHAP ID and CHAP response.

This brief discussion of RADIUS should be sufficient for this PPP book. Another book in this series has more information on RADIUS, and Chapter 9 explains the relationship of RADIUS and L2TP.

IPSec

The Internet Security Protocol (IPSec) will likely become the preferred protocol for providing secure tunnels through untrusted networks for user traffic. I say "likely" because IPSec is new and has not seen extensive deployment. Nonetheless, vendors and service providers are making plans for its deployment, and several Internet IETF working groups are developing standards for IPSec and how it supports other systems.

To begin the explanation of IPSec, we first need to clarify the concept of an IP secure tunnel in the context of how it is used in IPSec, see Figure 5–9. Broadly speaking, a secure tunnel conveys the idea of the secure transport of traffic between two systems across a nonsecure network (an untrusted network), or a single link. In this example, the Internet is a nonsecure network.

The actual passing of traffic is an instantiation of the security policies existing between the sending and receiving systems. The security policy (also referred to as meta-characteristics) include the addresses of the endpoints, an encapsulation method (by which the traffic is encapsulated inside other protocol data units), the cryptographic algorithms, the

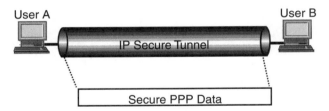

Figure 5–9   The IP secure tunnel

parameters for the algorithms (which include the size of the key and the lifetime of the key).

An IP secure tunnel refers to *all* the procedures, including protocols, encryption methods, etc. that ensure the safe passage of the traffic between the two systems. This set of capabilities is called a security association (SA). Be aware that a security association is not the secure tunnel itself, but an instantiation of the tunnel during a particular time, based on the SA.

We just learned that a security association defines a set of items (metacharacteristics) that is shared between two communicating entities. Its purpose is to protect the communications process between the parties.

An IPSec SA defines the following information as part of the security associations:

1. *Destination IP address.*
2. *Security protocol* that is to be used, which defines if the traffic is to be provided with integrity as well as secrecy support. It also defines the key size, key lifetime, and cryptographic algorithms (the algorithms are called transforms in IPSec).
3. *Secret keys* to be used by the cryptographic transforms.
4. *Encapsulation mode* (discussed in more detail later), which defines how the encapsulation headers are created and which part of the user traffic is actually protected during the communicating process.
5. *Security parameter index (SPI)* is the identifier of the SA. It provides information to the receiving device to know how to process the incoming traffic.

IPSec defines two types of IPSec mode SAs. I am going to quote directly from [KENT98c][2] in this part of the chapter to describe these modes, since their descriptions are best not left to a summary:

> A transport mode SA is a security association between two hosts. In IPv4, a transport mode security protocol header appears immediately after the IP header and any options, and before any higher layer protocols (e.g., TCP or UDP). In IPv6, the security protocol header appears after the base IP header and extensions, but may appear before or after destination options, and before higher layer protocols. In the case of ESP, a transport mode SA provides security services only for these higher layer protocols, not for the IP header or any extension headers preceding the ESP header. In the case of AH, the protection is also extended to selected portions of the IP header, selected portions of extension headers, and selected options (contained in the IPv4 header, IPv6 Hop-by-Hop extension header, or IPv6 Destination extension headers).
>
> A tunnel mode SA is essentially and SA applied to an IP tunnel. Whenever either end of a security association is a security gateway, the SA MUST be tunnel mode. Thus an SA between two security gateways is always a tunnel mode SA, as is an SA between a host and a security gateway. Note that for the case where traffic is destined for a security gateway, e.g., SNMP commands, the security gateway is acting as a host and transport mode is allowed. But in that case, the security gateway is not acting as a gateway, i.e., not transiting traffic. Two hosts MAY establish a tunnel mode SA between themselves. The requirement for any (transit traffic) SA involving a security gateway to be a tunnel SA arises due to the need to avoid potential problems with regard to fragmentation and reassembly of IPSec packets, and in circumstances where multiple paths (e.g., via different security gateways) exist to the same destination behind the security gateways.
>
> For a tunnel mode SA, there is an "outer" IP header that specifies the IPSec processing destination, plus an "inner" IP header that specifies the (apparently) ultimate destination for the packet. The security protocol header appears after the outer IP header, and before the inner IP header. If AH is employed in tunnel mode, portions of the outer IP header are afforded protection (as above), as well as all of the tunneled IP packet (i.e., all of the inner IP header is protected, as well as higher layer protocols). If ESP is employed, the protection is afforded only to the tunneled packet, not to the outer header.

IPSec and the AH and ESP Operations

IPSec uses two protocols to support user security operations. These protocols have not yet reached the final RFC standards stage. They are

---

[2][KENT98c] Kent, Stephen, "Security Architecture for the Internet Protocol," draft-ietf-ipsec-sec-07-txt., obsoletes RFC 1825, July 1998.

described in [KENT98a] for the IP Authentication Header (AH) and [KENT98b] for the IP Encapsulating Security Payload (ESP).[3] The use of two protocols is intended to provide choices in how traffic is protected and authenticated.

According to the specifications, the IP Authentication Header (AH) provides (a) integrity (called connectionless integrity in the specifications), (b) origin authentication, and (c) anti-replay services. The IP Encapsulating Security Payload (ESP) may provide: (a) confidentiality (encryption), (b) limited traffic flow confidentiality, (c) integrity, (d) origin authentication, and (e) anti-replay services. For ESP, one of these options must be implemented.

Both protocols are tools for access control, and may be used alone or applied in combination with each other. They support IPv4 or IPv6.

IPSec and L2TP

As discussed in Chapter 1, an important extension to PPP's services is the Layer-Two Tunneling Protocol (L2TP), which allows PPP to be extended across multiple links and networks. Obviously, this extension means that PPP traffic is more vulnerable to security breeches. Therefore, IPSec is also defined to support L2TP tunnels with IPSec tunnels. Before this operation is examined, it is necessary to first understand L2TP, then IPSec and L2TP can be explained. So, we must leave these discussions for Chapters 8 and 9.

OTHER REFERENCES

Two other security standards that deal with PPP may be of interest to you if you want to delve further into this subject. I refer you to: (a) G. Meyer, "The PPP Encryption Control Protocol (ECP)," RFC 1968, June 1996, and (b) K. Sklower, G. Meyer, "The PPP DES Encryption Protocol (DESE)," RFC 1969, June 1996.

---

[3][Kent98b] Kent, Steve and Atkinson, Randall, "IP Authentication Header," Internet Draft, July, 1998. [KENT98a], Kent, Steve and Atkinson, Randall, "IP Encapsulating Security Payload," July, 1998.

SUMMARY

Dial-in procedures, by their very nature, are vulnerable to security attacks. PPP defines an optional phase to deal with this problem. It is called the Authentication phase, and it is executed between the LCP and the NCP phases. While it is an option, most Internet systems employ it.

Several authentication protocols are used by PPP implementations to assure a user is indeed a legitimate user. CHAP is a common protocol used between the user and the NAS, and RADIUS is a common protocol used between the NAS and the RADIUS server.

6

Other PPP Operations

PP includes a wide variety and number of associated operations, options, and supporting protocols. Several warrant separate chapters, due to their breadth and complexity, and so are described in other chapters. This chapter examines the others.

I am not implying that by grouping these operations into one chapter, I am diminishing their importance. Indeed, some are used extensively in the PPP operations, and some are found in practically all vendor PPP products. The approach used here is simply a way to organize their descriptions.

RECOMMENDED EXTENSIONS

RFC 1662 recommends the following LCP options be implemented:

For high-speed links:

Magic Number
Link Quality Monitoring
No Address and Control Field Compression
No Protocol Field Compression

For low-speed or asynchronous links:

Async Control Character Map
Magic Number
Address and Control Field Compression
Protocol Field Compression

Vendor Extensions

In order to support proprietary protocols and systems on a PPP link, RFC 2153, *PPP Vendor Extensions*, defines LCP code 0. This extension also allows the implementation of various operations without their having to be registered through the Internet assigned numbers (RFC 1700). In order to set up this operation, an LCP or NCP packet is invoked with the code field set to zero.

Figure 6–1 shows the format of the vendor extension. The fields in this packet perform the following functions.

- *Code:* Set to 0 for vendor specific.
- *Identifier:* Used to identify uniquely each packet, and so must be changed for each packet.
- *Length:* Must be >= 12, and if the value is 12, the value field is not present.
- *Magic Number:* See the Magic-Number option in this chapter.
- *OUI:* The vendor's Organizational Unique Identifier, explained next in this section.
- *Kind:* Value in this field depends on the OUI.
- *Value(s):* As expected, this field or fields are implementation-specific.

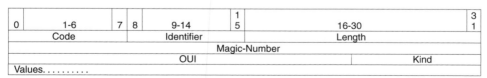

Note: Numbers at the top of the figure are the bit positions of the fields

Figure 6–1   Vendor-specific extension

0	1-6	7	8	9-14	1 5	16-30	3 1
Type			Length			OUI	
—			Kind			Values	
Values.							

Note: Numbers at the top of the figure are the bit positions of the fields

Figure 6–2   Configuration options

The Configuration Options that are placed in the PPP packet are quite limited, in fact, there is only one, the vendor-specific option. This option is coded as shown in Figure 6–2. The fields in this option were described in the discussion on the PPP packet (except the length field is >= 6).

THE OUI

The organizational unique identifier (OUI) is used widely throughout the data and voice communications industry to define vendor specific identifiers. Its genesis stems from the EtherType field in the Ethernet frame, and was enhanced with the publication of the IEEE 802 LAN standards. The reader who wishes more information on the assignment of the OUI can consult RFC 1700.

Also, RFC 2153 provides an option for the use of the OUI. If a vendor does not need a formally assigned number from the IEEE, it can use a PPP-specific OUI from the Internet assigned numbers.

MAXIMUM RECEIVE UNIT (MRU)

This option informs the receiving peer that the PPP can receive larger packets, or to request that the peer send smaller packets. The default value is 1,500 octets. If smaller packets are requested, an implementation should still be able to receive the full 1,500-octet information field in case link synchronization is lost.

ASYNCHRONOUS CONTROL CHARACTER MAP (ACCM)

This option allows an escape from the ASCII control characters 00–1F (the first two columns of the ASCII/IA5 code table) and defines a method to negotiate the use of control character transparency of asynchronous links. RFC 1662 provides information on this option. This next explanation is an extraction of RFC 1662.

Each end of the asynchronous link maintains two async-control character-maps. The receiving ACCM is 32 bits, but the sending ACCM may be up to 256 bits. This results in four distinct ACCMs, two in each direction of the link.

For asynchronous links, the default receiving ACCM is xFFFFFFFF. The default sending ACCM is xFFFFFFFF, plus the control Escape and Flag Sequence characters themselves, plus whatever the outgoing characters are flagged (by prior configuration) as likely to be intercepted.

The default inclusion of all octets less than hexadecimal 0x20 allows all ASCII control characters [6] excluding DEL (Delete) to be transparently communicated through all known data communications equipment.

The transmitter may also send octets with values in the range 0x40 through 0xFF (except x5E) in Control Escape format. Since these octet values are not negotiable, this does not solve the problem of receivers which cannot handle all noncontrol characters. Also, since the technique does not affect the eighth bit, this does not solve problems for communications links that can send only 7-bit characters.

However, it is rarely necessary to map all control characters, and often it is unnecessary to map any control characters. The Configuration Option is used to inform the peer which control characters must remain mapped when the peer sends them.

The peer may still send any other octets in mapped format, if necessary, because of constraints known to the peer. The peer should send a Configure-NAK packet with the logical union of the sets of mapped octets, so that when such octets are spuriously introduced they can be ignored on receipt.

Figure 6–3 shows the Async-Control-Character-Map Configuration Option format.

0	1-6	7	8	9-14	1 5	16-30	3 1
	Type			Length		ACCM	
ACCM continued							

Note: Numbers at the top of the figure are the bit positions of the fields

Figure 6–3   The ACCM option format

The type field is set to 2. The length field is set to 6. The ACCM field is four octets, and indicates the set of control characters to be mapped. The map is sent with the most significant octet first. Each numbered bit corresponds to the octet of the same value. If the bit is cleared to zero, then that octet need not be mapped. If the bit is set to one, then that octet *must* remain mapped. For example, if bit 19 is set to zero, then the ASCII control character 19 (DC3, Control-S) *may* be sent in the clear. The least significant bit of the least significant octet (the final octet transmitted) is numbered bit 0 and would map to the ASCII control character NUL.

AUTHENTICATION PROTOCOL

PPP sends the Configure-Request packet to indicate that it expects authentication from its peer. If an implementation sends a Configure-ACK, it is agreeing to authenticate with the specified protocol. An implementation receiving a Configure-ACK expects the peer to authenticate with the acknowledged protocol. See Chapter 5 for more detail information on this option.

QUALITY PROTOCOL

On some links, it may be desirable to determine when, and how often, the link is dropping data. This process is called link quality monitoring.

The implementation sending the Configure-Request indicates that it expects to receive monitoring information from its peer. If an implementation sends a Configure-ACK then it agrees to send the specified protocol. An implementation receiving a Configure-ACK expects the peer to send the acknowledge protocol.

MAGIC NUMBER

This option provides a method to detect looped-back links and other data-link layer problems, such as echoes. The Magic-Number is not negotiated, and zero is inserted where a Magic-Number might otherwise be used.

PPP chooses its Magic-Number in the most random manner possible in order to guarantee with very high probability that an implementation will arrive at a unique number.

When a Configure-Request is received with a Magic-Number Configuration Option, the received Magic-Number is compared with the Magic-Number of the last Configure-Request sent to the peer. If the two Magic-Numbers are different, then the link is not looped-back, and the Magic-Number is acknowledged. If the two Magic-Numbers are equal, then it is probable that the link is looped-back and that this Configure-Request is actually the one last sent. To determine this situation, a Configure-NAK is sent specifying a different Magic-Number value. A new Configure-Request is not sent to the peer until normal processing would cause it to be sent (that is, until a Configure-NAK is received or the Restart timer runs out).

PROTOCOL FIELD COMPRESSION (PFC)

This option provides a method to negotiate the compression of the PPP protocol field. By default, all implementations transmit packets with two octet PPP protocol fields.

PPP protocol field numbers are chosen such that some values may be compressed into a single octet form which is clearly distinguishable from the two octet form. This Configuration Option is sent to inform the peer that the implementation can receive such single octet protocol fields.

ADDRESS AND CONTROL FIELD COMPRESSION

This option provides a method to negotiate the compression of the Data Link Layer Address and Control fields. By default, all implementations transmit frames with address and control fields appropriate to the link framing.

Since these fields usually have constant values for point-to-point links, they are easily compressed. This Configuration Option is sent to inform the peer that the implementation can receive compressed Address and Control fields.

PPP AND LAPB

Let us return to the PPP LAPB option introduced in Chapter 2. The standard is published in RFC 1662 (PPP Reliable Transmission). LAPB uses an HDLC option called an asynchronous balanced mode (ABM) configuration. This configuration consists of two combined stations (the PPP peers) connected point-to-point only, half-duplex or full-duplex, switched or nonswitched. The combined stations have equal status on the channel and may send unsolicited frames to each other. Each station is equally responsible for link control. Typically, a station uses a command in order to solicit a response from the other station. The other station can send its own command as well. LAPB uses the balanced option of HDLC, but only on full-duplex, point-to-point links, which of course works well with PPP.

The term asynchronous has nothing to do with the format of the data or the physical interface of the stations. It is used to indicate that the stations need not receive a preliminary signal from another station before sending traffic. In other words, they can transmit without waiting on any other prior link-level signal. The industry uses the term *frame* to indicate the independent entity of data (protocol data unit) transmitted across the link from one station to another. The frame consists of four or five fields. The fields and the LAPB field sizes are as follows (also see Figure 6–4):

- Flag fields (F)   8 bits
- Address field (A)   8 or 16 bits (can be compressed)
- Control field (C)   8 or 16 bits (can be compressed)
- Information field (I)   variable length, not used in some frames
- Frame check sequence   16 or 32 bits
  field (FCS)

All frames must start and end with the flag (F) fields. The stations attached to the data link are required to continuously monitor the link for the flag sequence. The flag sequence consists of 01111110. Flags are transmitted on the link between HDLC frames to keep the link in an active condition. As such, they are known as *interframe* signals.

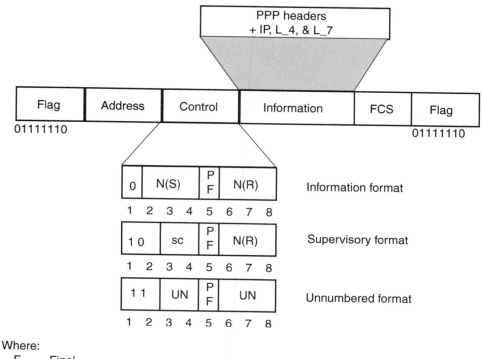

Where:
F   Final
FCS   Frame check sequence
N(R)   Receive number
N(S)   Send number
P   Poll
SC   Supervisory code
UN   Unnumbered

Figure 6–4   The PPP LAPB Option

The PPP Reliable Link Operations

The following material is provided as examples of PPP reliable link operations. Each figure shows the transmission of frames from station A to station B or from station B to station A. The term "station" refers to any type of machine that uses HDLC, such as a computer, a terminal, etc. HDLC is explained in more detail in Appendix A.

Each figure is accompanied by an explanation of the activities on the link. The arrows depict the time sequences of the frame transmissions.

The notation of "I" means the frame is carrying the information field. The P/F indicator is used to show if the poll/final (P/F) bit is set to 0 or 1. The N(S) and N(R) notations are used to show the values of the send and receive sequence numbers, respectively. The position of the fields in these figures do not show the order of field or bit transmission on the LAPB link. They are drawn to show the sequence of operations. Figure 6–5 shows the operation for a normal data transfer.

Event(s)	Operation
1	Station A sends an information frame and sequences the frame with N(S) = 0. The N(R) = 0 means station A is expecting to receive a frame with its field of N(S) = 0. The P

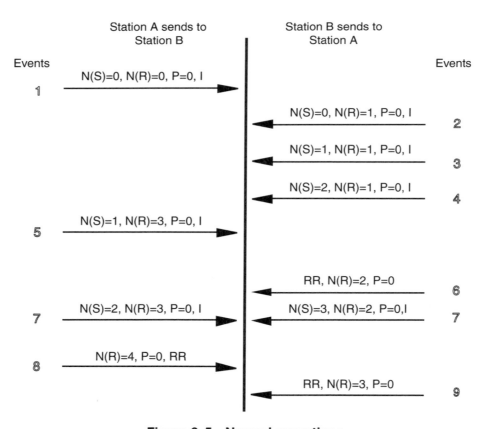

Figure 6–5   Normal operations

bit is set to 0, which means station A does not require station B to send any non-data frames.

2–4   Station B sends frames numbered N(S) = 0 through N(S) = 2. Its N(R) field is set to 1, which acknowledges station A's frame sent in event 1 [it had an N(S) value of 0].

5   Station A sends an I frame sequenced with N(S) = 1, which is the value station B expects next. Station A also sets the N(R) field to the value of 3, which inclusively acknowledges station B's previously transmitted frames numbered N (S) 0, 1, and 2.

6   Station B has no data to transmit. However, to prevent station A from "timing-out" and resending data, station B sends a receive ready (RR) frame.

7   The arrows depicting the frame flow from the two stations are aligned vertically with each other. This depiction means the two frames are transmitted from each station at about the same time and are exchanged almost simultaneously across the full-duplex link.

8–9   Stations A and B send RR frames to acknowledge the frames transmitted in event 7.

Figure 6–6 illustrates how LAPB uses its transmit (T1) timer. It also depicts how the P/F bit can be utilized to manage the flow of traffic between two stations.

Event(s)	Operation
1	Station A sends an I frame and sequences it with N(S) = 3.
2	Station B does not respond within the bounds of the T1 timer, so Station A times-out and sends a receive ready (RR) command frame with the P bit set to 1.
3	Station B responds with F = 1 and acknowledges station A's frame by setting N(R) = 4.
4	Station A resets T1 and sends another I frame. It sets the P bit set to 0 since the checkpoint is cleared.
5	Station B responds with an RR frame with N(R) = 5 and F = 0.

The events and operations to show error recovery with reject (REJ) are shown in Figure 6–7 and explained below.

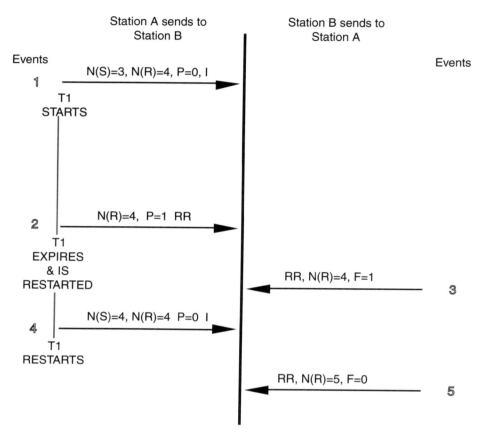

Figure 6–6   The T1 timer for retransmissions

Event(s)	**Operation**
1	Station A sends an I frame and sequences it with N(S) = 0. The N(R) = 0 means it expects station B to send an I frame with a send sequence number of 0.
2–5	Station B sends four frames numbered N(S) = 0, 1, 2, and 3. The N(R) value is set to 1 to acknowledge station A's previous frame. Notice the N(R) value does not change in any of these frames because station B is indicating that it is still expecting a frame from station A with a send sequence number of 1.
	During these frame transmissions, we assume that the frame with N(S) = 1 is distorted.

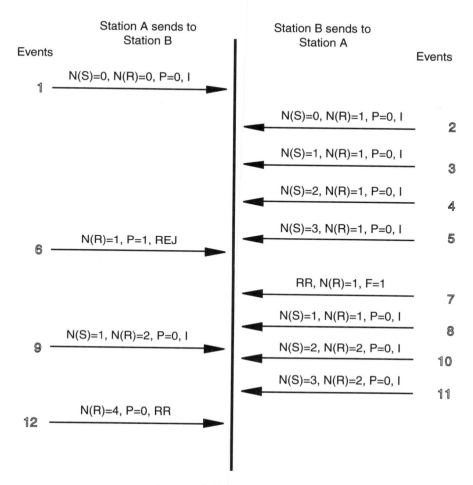

Figure 6–7   Error recovery

6   Station A issues a reject (REJ) frame with N(R) = 1 and
         P = 1. This means that it is rejecting station B's frame
         that was sequenced with the N(S) = 1, as well as all suc-
         ceeding frames.

7   Station B must first clear the P bit condition by sending a
         non-I frame with the F bit set to 1.

8–11   Station B then retransmits frames 1, 2, and 3. During
         this time (in event 9), station A sends an I frame with
         N(S) = 1. This frame has its N(R) = 2 to acknowledge the
         frame transmitted by station B in event 8.

12   Station A completes the recovery operations by acknowl-
       edging the remainder of station B's retransmissions.

RUNNING PPP OVER X.25

While X.25 is seeing diminished use, it is still quite prevalent in
many systems, and is often used as the transport bearer service for IP
and PPP traffic. RFC 1598 defines the procedures for running PPP over
X.25.

The X.25 virtual circuit can be a permanent virtual circuit (PVC), or
a switched virtual call (SVC). For PVCs, PPP is set up with the LCP procedures. For SVCs, the X.25 call management packets contain an encapsulation header that identifies that PPP encapsulation is being used on
the virtual circuit.

The PPP traffic is encapsulated into the X.25 data field. The control
information (headers and trailers) that are wrapped around PPP are
combinations of X.25's layer 2 (LAPB), and X.25's layer 3 (packet layer
procedures).[1]

RUNNING PPP OVER ISDN

RFC 1618 defines the rules for running PPP over ISDN. The ISDN
Primary Rate Interface (PRI), or the Basic Rate Interface (BRI) may support multiple concurrent B-channel links. The typical rates for the BRI
are: (a) one B channel with 64 kbit/s or (b) two B channels with 128
kbit/s. These are the rates that are usually made available to the PPP
dial-in user on a local loop from a residence to a service provider.

The PPP LCP and NCP mechanisms are useful in reducing or elimi-
nating manual configuration, and facilitating ease of communication between diverse implementations. The ISDN D-channel can also be used
for sending PPP packets when suitably framed, but it is limited in bandwidth (16 kbit/s) and often restricts communication links to a local
switch.

---

[1]It would have been simpler just to tunnel PPP transparently in the data field of
the L_3 packet, and leave the headers unaltered. But my point is moot, the RFC has
been this way since 1994.

RUNNING PPP OVER SONET

RFC 1619 defines the rules for running the PPP over SONET. Since SONET/SDH is a physical point-to-point circuit, PPP over SONET/SDH is a straightforward operation. This section paraphrases RFC 1619 (which is quite terse). See Figure 6–8 for a depiction of PPP in the SONET payload.

- PPP treats the SONET/SDH network as octet-oriented synchronous links.
- The PPP octet stream is mapped into the SONET/SDH synchronous payload envelope (SPE), with the PPP octet boundaries aligned with the SPE octet boundaries.
- Scrambling is not used.
- The path signal label (C2, located in the overhead area) is intended to indicate the contents of the SPE. The experimental value of 207 is used to indicate PPP.
- The multiframe indicator (H4, also located in the overhead area) is currently unused and must be zero.
- The basic rate for PPP over SONET/SDH is that of STS-3c/STM-1 at 155.520 Mbit/s.
- The available information bandwidth is 149.760 Mbit/s, which is the STS-3c/STM-1 SPE with section, line and path overhead removed. This operation is the same mapping used for ATM and FDDI.

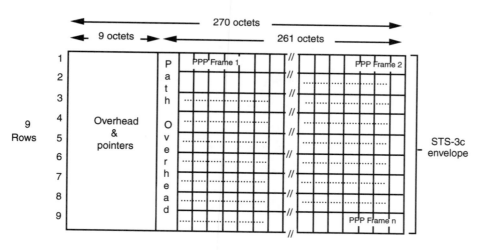

Figure 6–8   PPP Over SONET

LINK QUALITY MONITORING (LQM)

Some links are error-prone, subject to traffic loss and link outage. It is a good idea to have some means to monitor links in a network to test their quality and to take them out of commission, if necessary. Another possibility is to route traffic away from these troublesome links.

RFC 1989, the PPP Link Quality Monitoring (LQM) protocol, is designed to assist the network manager in the link monitoring and testing procedures. However, LQM makes no attempt to provide guidance on how the network manager deals with link problems. LQM lets you know if you have link problems; how you solve them is up to you.

Figure 6–9 introduces the major features of LQM. Like all the PPP operations, the use of LQM is negotiated with LCP during the link establishment. After the link is established and user traffic is flowing in an en-

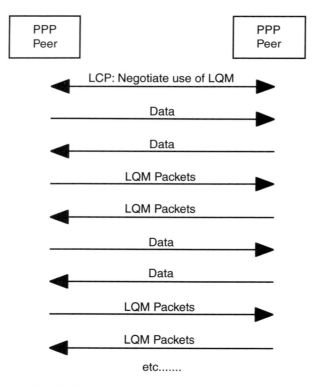

Figure 6–9   PPP link quality monitoring (LQM), RFC 1989

capsulated PPP frame (say, IP datagrams, identified with PPP Protocol ID x0021), LQM packets can be multiplexed periodically on the link. The data in these packets contain information on the number of packets/octets sent and received by the PPP peers, and some other useful values, such as Magic Number.

Consequently, the operational link now has both user and monitoring traffic on it. RFC 1989 requires that the LQM traffic be given precedence over user traffic, but this level of detail may be ignored.

Because of a standardized monitoring protocol, the PPP nodes know the exact meaning of the LQM statistics contained in the LQM packets. The counters used to report the LQM data are part of the RFC. But once again, how all this information is used is implementation-specific.

OTHER PPP PROCEDURES

FCS Alternatives

This option allows the use of a larger cyclic redundancy check (CRC) number for the PPP frame check sequence (FCS) field. The default value is 16 bits, which can be negotiated to 32 bits.

Self-Describing PAD

This option describes how padding octets are placed at the end of the PPP I field in order to place the field on a boundary convenient for processing.

Numbered Mode

This option uses X.25's L_2 LAPB, which provides for sequencing, ACKs, NAKs, and retransmissions of the PPP traffic. Earlier in this chapter, we examined LAPB in more detail.

Multilink Procedure

This option allows the grouping together of multiple single links. It is not needed now that multilink PPP (RFC 1990) is available (see Chapter 7).

DCE Identifier

This option allows the identification of specific DCEs, such as DSU or CSU. It is used by these devices to negotiate a subset of PPP features.

Multilink Plus Procedure

This option is based on Ascend's proprietary protocol.

Link Discriminator

This option is used to identify a single link in a multilink group. It is described in more detail in Chapter 7.

Network-Layer Protocols

PPP supports the encapsulation of several network-layer protocols in the PPP I field. They are:

- IPv4
- IPv6
- Internet packet exchange (IPX)
- NetBIOS
- Systems network architecture (SNA)
- OSI's connectionless network-layer protocol (CLNP)
- DECnet Phase IV
- Banyan Vines
- L_2 Bridges

Each network-layer protocol usually has two PPP protocol numbers. The first is used by NCP to negotiate the options for the protocol. These PPP protocol numbers range from hex 8000-BFFF. The second number identifies the protocol itself and is the same value as the NCP value less 8000. These protocols were also explained in Chapter 5.

SUMMARY

It is evident from this chapter alone that PPP and its related protocols offer a wide range of services to an internet user. Some are used extensively in the PPP operations and in vendor PPP products. When joined by these other supporting protocols, PPP becomes a powerful tool for user and network managers. As we move to the other chapters in this book, we will introduce yet more PPP services.

7

PPP Multilink Protocol (MP)

This chapter examines the PPP Multilink Protocol (MP). It explains how MP was derived from LAPB's Multilink Protocol (MLP). The MP header is examined as its contents reveal how MP manages the flow of traffic across multiple links while it insures that the traffic is properly sequenced at the receiver. The chapter concludes with an overview of the Bandwidth Allocation Protocol (BAP), which can be used to allocate and manage bandwidth on multilinks.

PURPOSE OF THE MULTILINK PROTOCOL (MP)

The PPP Multilink Protocol (MP) defines the procedures for using multiple links between two PPP nodes, such as an end user and a service provider. It defines the methods for splitting packets across multiple links, and recombining them at the end node. While it was developed to be used on multiple-bearer ISDN channels, it can be applied to any set of links. MP is published as RFC 1990, which obsoletes RFC 1717.

In recent years, many manufacturers have developed link-level protocols to manage more than one link. The advantages are obvious. First, additional throughput can be achieved; second, a faulty link can be replaced by a predefined back-up link. As just mentioned, RFC 1990 was conceived to exploit ISDN's multiple-bearer channels (B channels), but it is applicable to any system that has multiple links and channels.

MODEL FOR MP

The ISO publishes a standard for multilink procedures in ISO 7776, and in 1984, LAPB was amended to include provisions for multilink procedures (MLP). The MLP protocol is quite similar to SNA's transmission group and SS7's link set. Figure 7–1 shows the arrangement for LAPB's (Link Access Procedure, Balanced) MLP, from which both the PPP multilink procedure as well as ISO 7776 were derived.

In an MLP configuration, stations communicate through more than one communications link, shown in this figure as physical links 1, 2, and n. Each single-link channel behaves just as we have learned earlier. Basically, MLP adds two additional components: a sequence number for all

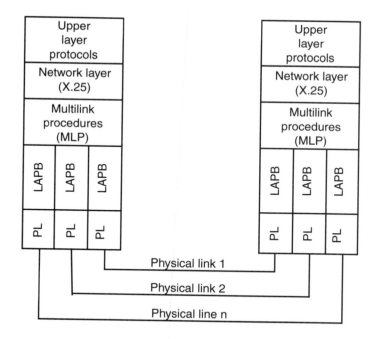

Where:
LAPB   Link access procedure, balanced
PL   Physical layer (L_1)

Figure 7–1   Multilink LAPB: Basis for PPP multilink protocol

the multilinks; and indicators about the beginning, continuation, or end-ing of a packet. This sequence number is used to manage the windows and flow control across all the links that are identified to the multilink. The LAPB multilink sequence number ranges from 0 to 4095 in order to accommodate many links operating at high data transfer rates.

The flow control, sequencing, and window management of MLP closely follow the concepts of individual single links. The main difference is MLP's management of the multiple physical links as if they were one logical link (called a bundle).

Nonetheless, each link is controlled by a single-link protocol, PPP's rendition of HDLC. The receiving single-link protocols only deliver the protocol data units (PDUs, or frames) to the MLP sublayers when the FCS error-check passes and all edits on the control fields are satisfac-tory. Then, the MLP sublayer resequences the data before sending it to its next upper layer (usually, the network layer).

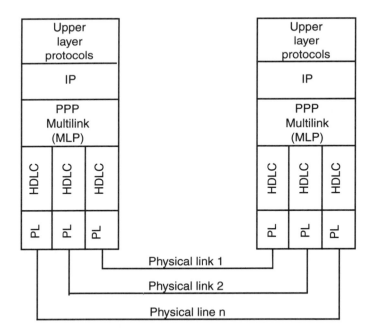

Where:
HDLC   High Level Data Link Control
PL   Physical layer (L_1)

Figure 7–2   PPP multilink protocol layered structure

The PPP MP Approach

The PPP multilink protocol (MP) is quite similar to the multilink protocol described in ISO 7776 and the multilink procedures found in LAPB; the MP configuration is shown in Figure 7–2. One difference between MP and the international standards is that there is no requirement for acknowledged-mode operation on the link layer, although it is permitted as an option. MP is based on an LCP option negotiation that permits a system to indicate to its peer that it is capable of combining multiple physical links into a "bundle."

MP NEGOTIATION DURING LCP OPERATIONS

MP is negotiated during the initial LCP option negotiation. A node indicates to its peer that it is willing to support multilink operations by sending the multilink option as part of the initial LCP option negotiation. This negotiation indicates three things: (a) The system is capable of MP; (b) it is capable of fragmenting upper layer PDUs; and (c) it is capable of receiving PDUs that are larger than the maximum receive unit (MRU) for one physical link.

So, MP coordinates multiple independent links between a fixed pair of nodes (point-to-point). The bundle (aggregate link in MLP terminology [a link set, or trunk group in other technologies]) is named by the pair of identifiers for the two nodes connected by the multiple links. A system identifier may include information provided by PPP Authentication and information provided by LCP negotiation.

MP is flexible. The bundled links can be different physical links, such as multiple async lines, or they may be instances of multiplexed links, such as ISDN, X.25 or Frame Relay. The links may also be of different types, such as dialup async links or leased synchronous links.

RULES ON THE USE OF PPP OPTIONS

RFC 1990 establishes rules regarding the use of PPP options, and states that these options are manually configured for MP operations:

- No Async Control Character Map (ACCM)
- No Magic Number
- No Link Quality Monitoring

- Has Address and Control Field Compression
- No Compound Frames
- No Self-Describing-Padding

Each link is allowed to have different values for these options, but LCP negotiations cannot be performed on the MP bundle. In addition, the LCP configure and terminate packets cannot be sent through the multilink procedure. Other packets that do not change the default settings are permitted. Those LCP packets are: (a) Code-Reject, (b) Protocol-Reject, (c) Echo-Request, (d) Echo-Reply, and (e) Discard-Request.

If any network layer packets are sent across the bundle without the MP services, they are not sequenced and may arrive out of order.

CONFIGURATION OPTIONS

MP defines three configuration options. They are:

- *Multilink maximum received reconstructed unit.* This option indicates the sending peer supports the PPP Multilink Protocol. The data field in this option specifies the maximum number of bytes that can be in the reassembled fragments. The node must be able to receive at least 1,500 octets, although it might try to negotiate a smaller (or larger) value
- *Multilink short sequence number header format.* This option indicates the peer desires to receive fragments with a 12-bit (short) sequence number. The option pertains to all links in the bundle. If this option is not negotiated, the default 24-bit sequence number is used.
- *Endpoint discriminator.* This option identifies the system that is sending the traffic. It informs the receiver of the nature of the address assignment (local, IEEE, etc.), and the address itself.

PACKET FORMATS

Figure 7–3 shows the layout of individual fragments, which are the packets in the Multilink Protocol. Network Protocol packets are first encapsulated (but not framed) according to normal PPP procedures, and

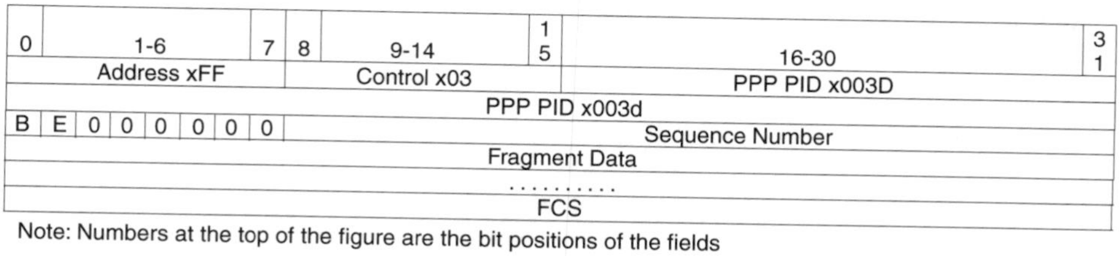

0	1-6	7	8	9-14	15	16-30	31
	Address xFF			Control x03		PPP PID x003D	
				PPP PID x003d			
B	E 0 0 0 0 0 0					Sequence Number	
				Fragment Data			
				. . . .			
				FCS			

Note: Numbers at the top of the figure are the bit positions of the fields

Figure 7–3   The Multilink Protocol (MP) protocol data unit

large packets are broken up into multiple segments, sized appropriately for the multiple physical links.

A new PPP header consisting of the Multilink Protocol Identifier of x003D, and the Multilink header is inserted before each section. (Thus the *first* fragment of a multilink packet in PPP will have two headers—one for the fragment, followed by the header for the packet itself).

This format shows a sequence number of 24 bits. Another option (not shown) uses a 12-bit sequence number. The B bit (Beginning bit) is set to 1 on the first fragment of the original PPP packet, and to 0 on all other fragments of this PPP packet. The E bit (Ending bit) is set to 1 on the last fragment of the original PPP packet and 0 on all other fragments.

The FCS field is a conventional HDLC field that is computed on each fragment. No error check is performed on the complete PPP packet.

Example of MP Operations

MP is a flexible specification regarding fragmentation, and MP nodes are not required to fragment small packets. There is no requirement that the segments be of equal sizes, or that packets must be fragmented.

The fragments are encapsulated using the protocol identifier x003D. Following the protocol identifier is a 4-byte header containing a sequence number, and two 1-bit fields indicating that the fragment begins (B bit) a packet or terminates (E bit) a packet. After negotiating an additional PPP LCP option, the 4-byte header may be optionally replaced by a 2-byte header with only a 12-bit sequence space.

Figure 7–4 shows an example of how the MP operates with the B, E, and sequence number fields. The B bit is a 1-bit field set to 1 on the first fragment derived from a PPP packet and set to 0 for all other fragments from the same PPP packet. The E bit is a 1-bit field set to 1 on the last fragment and set to 0 for all other fragments. A fragment may have both

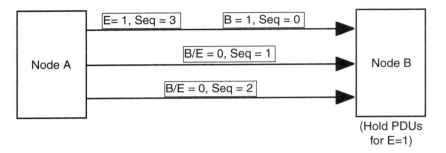

Figure 7–4   Example of multilink operations

the B and E bits set to 1. For each fragment received from a PPP packet, the receiver keeps track of the received sequence numbers. Upon receiving the fragment with E set to 1, it checks to make certain all sequence numbers have been received.

RFC 1990 stipulates these rules for the fragmentation operations, and the detection of lost fragments:

- For each member link in the bundle, the sender must increase the sequence number for each fragment.
- The sequence number cannot be reset for each new PPP packet; the number is simply a wrap-around counter for the bundle.
- The sequence number starts at 0 for a new bundle, so the addition of a link to an existing bundle is invisible to MP.
- A lost fragment is detected when not all the sequence numbers between the B and E bit fragments have been received.

Example of Fragment-Loss Detection

We learned that the sequence field is a 24-bit or 12-bit number that is incremented for every fragment transmitted. By default, the sequence field is 24 bits long, but can be negotiated to be only 12 bits with an LCP configuration option. A single reassembly structure is associated with the bundle.

We also learned that the sender transmits fragments with the sequence numbers incremented on each member link in a bundle. The receiver detects lost fragments based on a comparison of sequence numbers. Recall that the sequence number is not reset upon each new PPP packet, and a sequence number is consumed even for those fragments

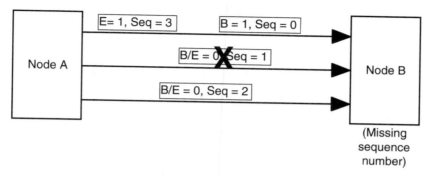

Figure 7–5   Error detection

which contain an entire PPP packet, i.e., one in which both the beginning (B) and ending (E) bits are set to 1.

The other rules in RFC 1990 for fragment loss detection are: (1) The receiver keeps track of the incoming sequence numbers on each link in a bundle. (2) It maintains the current minimum of the most recently received sequence number over all the member links in the bundle (the M variable). (3) The receiver detects the end of a packet when it receives a fragment with E = 1. (4) Reassembly of the packet is complete if all sequence numbers (up to that fragment) have been received.

A lost fragment is detected when M advances past the sequence number of a fragment bearing an E bit of a packet which has not been completely reassembled (i.e., not all the sequence numbers between the fragment bearing the B bit and the fragment bearing the E bit have been received). This situation is shown in Figure 7–5.

GUIDANCE ON BUFFER-SPACE REQUIREMENTS

RFC 1990 provides a useful explanation for the PPP peer's buffer-space requirements. Since this explanation does not lend itself to a summary, I quote directly from RFC 1990, Section 4.2:

> There is no amount of buffering that will guarantee correct detection of fragment loss, since an adversarial peer may withhold a fragment on one channel and send arbitrary amounts on the others. For the usual case where all channels are transmitting, you can show that there is a minimum amount below which you could not correctly detect packet loss. The amount depends on the relative delay between the channels, (D[channel-i,channel-j]), the data rate of

each channel, R[c], the maximum fragment size permitted on each channel, F[c], and the total amount of buffering the transmitter has allocated amongst the channels.

When using PPP, the delay between channels could be estimated by using LCP echo request and echo reply packets. (In the case of links of different transmission rates, the round trip times should be adjusted to take this into account.) The slippage for each channel is defined as the bandwidth times the delay for that channel relative to the channel with the longest delay, S[c] = R[c] * D[c,c-worst]. (S[c-worst] will be zero, of course!)

A situation which would exacerbate sequence number skew would be one in which there is extremely bursty traffic (almost allowing all channels to drain), and then where the transmitter would first queue up as many consecutively numbered packets on one link as it could, then queue up the next batch on a second link, and so on. Since transmitters must be able to buffer at least a maximum-sized fragment for each link (and will usually buffer up at least two) A receiver that allocates any less than S[1] + S[2] + ... + S[N] + F[1] + ... + F[N], will be at risk for incorrectly assuming packet loss, and therefore, SHOULD allocate at least twice that.

PROTOCOL EXTENSIONS

It is possible to achieve more reliable multilink operations by implementing the link access procedure balanced (LAPB) protocol, which is discussed in Chapter 6. We shall not deal with it further here except to note that if LAPB is to be used, it must be negotiated prior to the use of the multilink protocol. In addition, LAPB must be negotiated on each member link of the multilink bundle. Even if LAPB is not used in MP and an error is detected, the NCP operating on top of MP must be notified.

Compression may also be used with MP. Compression is negotiated and applied for each member link in the bundle, or alternately compression can be run over each bundle.

MP CONFIGURATION OPTION TYPES

The MP supports the use of three additional LCP configuration options:

- Multilink maximum received reconstructed unit
- Multilink short sequence number header format
- Endpoint discriminator

The next section describes each of these LCP Configuration Options.

Figure 7–6   Multilink MRRU LCP option

Multilink Maximum Received Reconstructed Unit (MRRU)

When the sender places the MRRU option in a PPP packet, it tells the receiver that the sender is implementing the PPP multilink protocol. Figure 7–6 shows the format for the MRRU LCP option. It consists of the type field which is set to 17, the link field set to 4 and the max-received-reconstructed unit field which is two octets. This latter field defines the maximum number of octets that will be contained in the information fields (I fields) of reassembled packets. In keeping with other operations of PPP, a PPP peer must be able to receive a 1,500-octet information field, although MP permits negotiation of a smaller or larger I field size.

The multilink protocol RFC defines a number of rules pertaining to how the MRRU LCP option is implemented. These rules are beyond this general treatise and I refer you to Section 5-.1.1 of RFC 1990 if you wish more details on this option.

Short Sequence Number Header Format Option

As its name implies, the Short Sequence Number Header Format Option is used to inform the peer PPP that the sending peer desires to receive fragments with short (12-bit) sequence numbers. Upon an acknowledgement of this option, the peer then must transmit all multilink packets on all links of the bundle with a 12-bit sequence number, otherwise it must send a Configure-Reject a packet back to the initial sender. The default field for multilink protocol operations is a 24-bit sequence number. Consequently, if this option is not negotiated, the sequence number will be 24 bits for the duration of the bundle. The format for this LCP option is quite simple as depicted in Figure 7–7. It consists of the type field equal to 18 and a link field of 2.

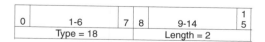

Figure 7–7   Short sequence number header format option

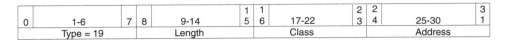

0	1-6	7	8	9-14	1 5	1 6	17-22	2 3	2 4	25-30	3 1
	Type = 19			Length			Class			Address	

Figure 7–8   Endpoint discriminator option

Endpoint Discriminator Option

The endpoint discriminator option coding is depicted in Figure 7–8.

It is identified with type-19, a link field, a class field, and an address field. The purpose of this option is to identify the system that is transmitting the PPP packet. In essence, it tells the receiver that the peer on this link might be the same as the peer on another existing link, or it might be different.

PPP BANDWIDTH ALLOCATION PROTOCOL (BAP) AND BANDWIDTH ALLOCATION CONTROL PROTOCOL (BACP)

The BAP and BACP were introduced into the industry as a means to support the dynamic allocation of bandwidth on PPP multilinks. Both protocols are described in RFC 2125.

BAP is used to manage the number of links in a multilink bundle and defines the procedures to add or remove links in the bundle. BACP is the associated control protocol for BCP.

RFC 2125 calls its overall operations bandwidth-on-demand (BOD). However this definition of BOD is different from other technologies, such as Frame Relay and ATM. With these systems, BOD means that traffic is "shaped" on an existing link to provide the needed bandwidth. With BAP/BACP, BOD means the allocation or removal of links in a multilink bundle to change the capacity (bandwidth) of the bundle. This change can occur dynamically during the ongoing multilink connection.

An example of how BAP can be used is to set up another link in a bundle by one PPP node informing its peer with a BAP request packet. The receiving PPP node can then add this link to its bundle, associate a phone number with it, and then inform the application of the availability of the new link. After these operations are performed, the receiver can send back a response to the sender indicating that the link is placed in an operational mode.

The LCP Configuration Option is used for these operations. The LCP option is 23 (the Link Discriminator Option). BACP uses the same operations as LCP (described in Chapter 4). The PPP protocol field is set to xC02B to identify the Bandwidth Allocation Control Protocol, and xC02D to identify the Bandwidth Allocation Protocol.

These protocols interact with PPP and each other in the following manner: (a) PPP must have reached the Network (Layer) Control Phase before any BAP packets can be exchanged, and (b) BACP must have reached the opened state before BAP can operate.

BACP Operations

BACP is executed first to allow the negotiation of parameters between the MP peers. Currently, there is only one parameter, called the favored-peer. This configuration option is used in the event that the two peers transmit the same BAP request (a race condition). The Magic Number field is used to resolve the race condition.

BAP Operations

BAP defines the procedures to allow two endpoints to negotiate the adding and dropping links from a multilink bundle. The BAP implementation can do the following:

- Request permission to add a link to a bundle (Call-Request).
- Request that the peer add a link to a bundle via a callback (Callback-Request).
- Negotiate the dropping of a link from a bundle (Link-Drop-Query-Request).

Once BACP has reached its opened state, a peer can request another link be added to the bundle by sending a BAP Call- or a Callback-Request packet. A Call-Request packet is sent if the implementation wishes to originate the call for the new link, and a Callback-Request packet is sent if the implementation wishes its peer to originate the call for the new link. The implementation receiving a Call- or Callback-Request must respond with a valid response code in the Call- or Callback-Response packet.

Of course, a link may also be dropped from a bundle. This operation uses a BAP Link-Drop-Query-Request packet, which is sent to the peer to negotiate the dropping of a link. The peer must respond with a Link-Drop-Query-Response. If the peer is agreeable to dropping the link the implementation must issue an LCP a Terminate-Request packet to initiate dropping the link. More detailed information on BAP can be obtained in RFC 2125.

SUMMARY

The PPP multilink protocol is used to manage multiple links as a logical whole. It defines the methods for splitting packets across multiple links, and recombining them at the receiving node. MP manages the flow of traffic across these links and insures the traffic is properly sequenced at the receiver. MP can also detect the loss of traffic, but it does not define what actions to take to recover from the loss.

BACP acts as the control program to BAP, which defines the packets (and formats) to achieve bandwidth operations. It also stipulates how links are dropped and how links are identified within the bundle.

8

Layer-Two Tunneling
Protocol (L2TP)

This Chapter introduces the Layer-2 Tunneling Protocol (L2TP). We explore why L2TP was developed, its benefit to the network manager, and how it is deployed in an internet. Because of L2TP's usefulness, it is finding increased use in many systems such as ATM and frame relay, and we cover those aspects of L2TP that deal with these technologies.

This discussion is based on [TOWN99],[1] which is an Internet draft document. As always, remember that these drafts are works-in-progress, and subject to change.

PURPOSE OF L2TP

We learned in Chapter 1 that L2TP was introduced to the industry to allow the use of the PPP procedures between different networks and multiple communications links. In essence, with L2TP, PPP is extended as an encapsulation and negotiation protocol to allow the transport of PPP and user traffic between different networks and nodes.

---

[1][TOWN99] Townsley, W.M., et al., "Layer Two Tunneling Protocol, L2TP," Network Working Group, Internet-Draft, draft-ietf-pppext-15.txt, May 1999.

One principal reason for the advent of L2TP is the need to dial in to a network access server (NAS) that may reside at a remote location. While this NAS may be accessed through the dial-up link, which has been the focus of the explanations in this book thus far, it may be that the NAS is located in another network. L2TP allows the use of all the PPP operations we have covered in this book to be used between machines in different networks.

With the implementation of L2TP, an end user establishes a layer-2 connection to an access concentrator such as a modem bank, an ADSL bank, etc. Thereafter, the concentrator is responsible for creating a tunnel and sending the specific PPP packets to a network access server (NAS).

The idea of L2TP is to "elevate" the visibility of PPP across multiple links and multiple networks. Consequently, L2TP does not concern itself with a link-to-link operation. Rather, it concerns itself with logical point-to-point operations across multiple links and multiple networks.

BENEFITS OF L2TP

Prior to the advent of L2TP, the capabilities just explained were being developed in a proprietary fashion. For example, Microsoft developed the Point-to-Point Tunneling Protocol (PPTP) and Cisco developed the Layer-2 Forwarding Protocol (L2FP). The value to users of L2TP is that it is a standard that encompasses the attributes of these proprietary protocols.

L2TP provides a number of useful services to data network users. First, multiple protocols can be supported and negotiated, although IP is the prevalent protocol. L2TP also allows the use of unregistered IP addresses through the use of tunnels. A NAS can be used to assign addresses from a single address pool, thus simplifying the IP address management process. L2TP also permits the centralization of login and authentication operations by co-locating a NAS with an L2TP Access Concentrator (LAC). L2TP allows a virtual dial-up service where many autonomous system protocol domains are able to share access to core infrastructure components such as routers, modems, and access servers.

TERMINOLOGY DEALING WITH L2TP

Before we begin a detailed analysis of L2TP, it will be helpful to define several terms (see Figure 8–1). It is suggested you read these terms before you read the analysis of L2TP.

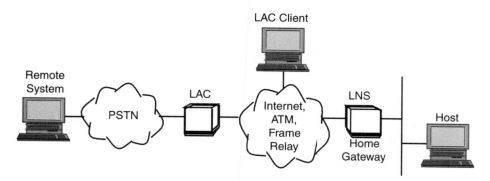

Figure 8–1   The L2TP configuration

- *L2TP Network Server (LNS):* The LNS is a node acting at one side of the peer L2TP tunnel endpoint. Its other peer is the L2TP Access Concentrator (LAC), discussed next. The LNS is the termination point of a PPP session that is being tunneled from the LAC.
- *L2TP Access Concentrator (LAC):* The LAC is the other side of the L2TP tunnel, and it is the peer to the LNS described in the paragraph above. The LAC resides between the LNS and a remote system. Its job is to forward traffic to and from the LAC and the end system. The LAC is responsible for tunneling and detunneling operations between the user and the LNS.
- *L2TP Tunnel:* This tunnel exists between the LAC and LNS peers. It consists of the user traffic and the header information necessary to support the tunnel. Therefore, the tunnel provides the encapsulated PPP packets and the requisite control messages needed for the operations between the LAC and LNS.

HOW THE COMPONENTS FIT TOGETHER

In Figure 8–1, we see the placement of the LAC and the LNS in regards to the public switch telephone network (PSTN), the Internet, and possibly a Frame Relay or ATM network. The basic concept of L2TP is for a remote system to initiate a PPP connection through the PSTN to a LAC. The job of this LAC is to tunnel the PPP connection through the Internet and perhaps through a Frame Relay or ATM network to a local LNS. At this LNS, a home LAN is discovered. After the discovery process is completed, the traffic is delivered to the end user via the "tunnel."

THE L2TP TUNNEL AND TUNNEL SESSIONS

L2TP tunnels are named by identifiers that have local significance only at each end of the tunnel. The same tunnel will be given different tunnel IDs by each end of the tunnel. The tunnel ID in each message is that of the intended recipient, not the sender. Tunnel IDs are selected and exchanged as assigned tunnel ID AVPs (attribute value pairs, a syntax convention, discussed shortly) during the creation of a tunnel.

L2TP allows different sets of PPP peer terminals to utilize one tunnel via session operations. L2TP sessions exist within tunnels and are named by identifiers that have local significance, like that of tunnel IDs. The session ID in each message is that of the intended recipient, not the sender. Session IDs are also selected and exchanged as assigned session ID AVPs during the creation of a session.

Figure 8–2 shows the idea of the L2TP tunnel and the sessions associated with the tunnel. The tunnel extends between the LAC and the LNS through an internet such as an ATM network, a Frame Relay network, or even the telephone network. Figure 8–2 shows three sessions in operation through the tunnel. One session supports nodes A and D; another session supports nodes B and E, and the third session supports

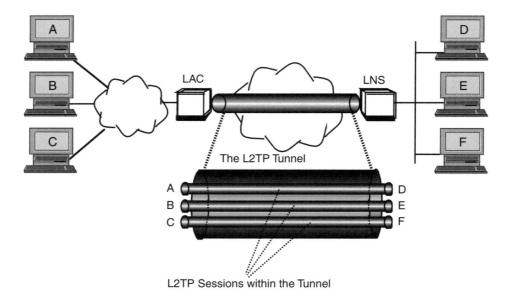

Figure 8–2   The L2TP tunnel and tunnel sessions

nodes C and F. In many situations, the tunnel will not connect to two end users, but an end user and a server.

THE L2TP MESSAGES

To establish communications between different endpoints across multiple links or networks, L2TP uses two different types of messages. One message type is called a control message and the other is called a data message. As the names imply, the control messages are used to set up, maintain, and clear L2TP tunnels between nodes. Data messages of course are used to encapsulate the PPP packets into the tunnel and correctly identify them for transport between the two nodes. We shall see that the control messages are supported with a reliable control procedure to insure the safe delivery, whereas, as you might expect by now, in the reading of this book, the data messages are subject to loss if errors should occur.

THE L2TP PROTOCOL STACK

Figure 8–3 shows the L2TP protocol stack arrangement. The underlying bearer technology shown in this figure as transport services consists of a typical network such as ATM and Frame Relay. The figure also

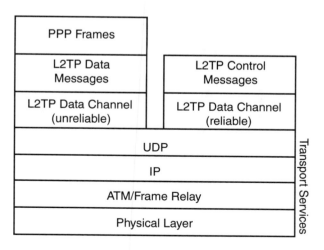

Figure 8–3   The L2TP protocol stack

shows the placement of the data and control messages in regards to the protocol stack. L2TP runs on top of UDP and is identified with port 1701. Just like other UDP operations, the initiator of the operation selects an available source port number and places this number in the source port field of the UDP header. The destination port number is set to 1701. The receiver of this datagram notes the port numbers in the UDP header.

The receiver's reply does not require the use of port 1701. The destination port number is the same as the source port number in the incoming UDP header, and the source port number is one chosen by the receiver for the reply. Hereafter, the port numbers must remain the same for the duration of the session.

The L2TP approach is different from many systems in how the ports are chosen. Usually, the port numbers are simply reversed. The absence of the well-known port (1701) might create problems in the future in networks that use well-known port numbers to assign labels or provide tailored services.

THE L2TP HEADER AND MESSAGES (AVPs)

A common header is used for both the control channel and the data channel transmissions. Figure 8–4 shows the format of this header.

The fields in the header perform the following functions:

- *Type (T) bit:* Indicates type of message (0 for a data message and 1 for a control message).
- *Length (L) bit:* Indicates that a Length field is present.
- *X bits:* Reserved for future extensions.
- *Sequence (S) bit:* Set to 1 to indicate sequence numbers are present (the sequence number fields are Ns and Nr, discussed later). Sequence numbers are required for control messages, and operate in the conventional manner of most sequencing protocols.

0	1-10	1 1	12-14	1 5	16-30	3 1
T	L x x S x O P x x x x		Ver		Length (opt)	
	Tunnel ID				Session ID	
	Ns (opt)				Nr (opt)	
	Offset Size (opt)				Offset Pad . . . (opt)	

Figure 8–4   The L2TP common header

- *Offset (O) bit:* Indicates if the Offset Size field is present, a requirement for control messages.
- *Priority (P) bit:* Indicates if this data message should receive preferential treatment in its local queuing and transmission. For example, LCP messages can be used as pings for keep-alive operations. The P-bit usage would be helpful for this type of traffic.
- *Version (Ver):* Set to 2 for the current version of L2TP.
- *Length field:* Indicates the total length of message in octets.
- *Tunnel ID:* Indicates the identifier for the control connection.
- *Session ID:* Indicates the identifier for a session within a tunnel.
- *Ns:* Indicates the sequence number for this data or control message beginning at zero and incrementing by one (modulo 2^{16}) for each message sent.
- *Nr:* Indicates the sequence number expected in the next control message to be received. Nr is set to the Ns of the last in-order message received plus one (modulo 2^{16}). In data messages, Nr is reserved and, if present (as indicated by the S-bit), is ignored upon receipt.
- *Offset Size:* Specifies the number of octets past the L2TP header at which the payload data is expected to start.
- *Offset Pad:* Pads the bits to an even 32-bit alignment.

THE FIELDS FOLLOWING THE HEADER

The syntax of the fields following the header is called the Attribute Value Pair (AVP). AVPs are simply a means of establishing a standard for representing L2TP traffic. The AVP consists of an attribute value, which is represented by an integer and followed by a value that contains the actual message itself. Typically, multiple AVPs are coded behind the header to be exchanged between the LAC and the LNS. In the next section of this chapter, we look at some examples of the coding of the AVPs.

The AVPs

This section provides a summary of the L2TP AVPs. They all share a common coding format, shown in Figure 8–5. The fields in this message perform the following functions:

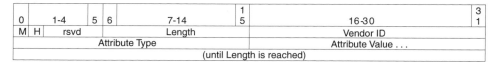

0	1-4	5	6	7-14	1 5	16-30	3 1
M	H	rsvd		Length		Vendor ID	
Attribute Type					Attribute Value . . .		
(until Length is reached)							

Figure 8–5   The AVP format

- *M (Mandatory) bit:* If this bit is set, and the receiver cannot recognize a AVP in the message, it must terminate the session in the tunnel or the entire tunnel, depending upon the nature of the AVP. If the bit is not set, an unrecognized AVP is ignored.
- *H (Hidden) bit:* Indicates the hiding of data in the Attribute Value field of an AVP. The hiding of data entails the use of encryption and implies that each end of the tunnel share the same secret to enable the authentication of the traffic. I refer you to Section 4.2 of [TOWN99] for the details of hash function performed on hidden data.
- *Length:* Indicates the length of the entire AVP.
- *Vendor ID:* This field is set to 0 for standardized AVP values, and to the vendor-specific number (RFC 1700) for proprietary AVP values.
- *Attribute Type:* A unique value of each AVP within the Vendor ID.
- *Attribute Value:* The actual value (the data in the AVP), as indicated by the Vendor ID and the Attribute Type.

AVP Categories

The AVPs are grouped into six categories, based on their functions and characteristics. These categories are described next, and Tables 8–1 to 8–6 provide summaries of each AVP within its respective category. The attribute type (value) is listed with the name of the AVP in the first column in these tables. The six categories are:

- AVPs that are appplicable to all control messages
- AVPs pertaining to result and error codes
- AVPs pertaining to control connection management
- AVPs pertaining to call management
- AVPs pertaining to LCP negotiation and authentication
- AVPs pertaining to the status of calls

Table 8–1   AVPs for all control messages

AVP Type (Value)	Function of AVP
Message Type (0)	Type of AVP message
Random Vector (36)	Used in hiding operation. Contains hash vector for hash function.

Only two AVPs are applicable to all control messages, and they are listed and summarized in Table 8–1. The Message Type identifies the type of AVP message. AVP type 36, the Random Vector, is used in the authentication procedures, and described in Chapter 5.

Table 8–2 provides a summary of the sole AVP associated with result and error codes, which is called the Result Code. Notice that two types of "diagnostic" codes are used by L2TP. The Result Code represents a severe event in which the control channel or the session is terminated. The Error Code does not terminate a session or a channel, but informs the sender of the traffic that the receiver cannot translate or decode (or chooses not to) one or more parameters in the message.

Table 8–3 lists and provides a summary of the AVPs associated with control connection management. A few comments are in order about some of these AVPs. Like PPP, L2TP accepts asynchronous or synchronous framing (AVP type 3). AVP type 4 allows the peer to define if the hardware interface for the sender is analog or digital. The tie-breaker AVP (value 5) is used to resolve a situation where both the LAC and LNS simultaneously set up a tunnel. The procedure defines how one of the peers drops its tunnel. The receive window AVP (value 10) is used to inform the peer of the number of messages the receiver can receive without message loss (in essence, the receive buffer size).

Table 8–4 shows lists and provides a summary of the AVPs associated with Call Management. Recall that L2TP first sets up a connection between the peers, then it sets up calls, based on the user's calls to the

Table 8–2   AVP for result and error codes

AVP Type (Value)	Function of AVP
Result Code (1)	Result Code: Indicates reason for terminating a control channel or session. Examples: (a) wrong version of protocol, (b) busy signal at called party, (c) authentication failure.
	Error Code: Indicates problems with protocol or message formats and contents

Table 8–3   AVPs for control connection management

AVP Type (Value)	Function of AVP
Protocol Version (2)	Indicates protocol version of sender of the message
Framing Capabilities (3)	Indicates to peer the acceptance of synchronous or asynchronous framing of the traffic
Bearer Capabilities (4)	Indicates to peer the support of analog or digital access
Tie Breaker (5)	Used to resolve the simultaneous set up of a new tunnel between peers
Firmware Revision (6)	Indicates firmware revision of the sender of the message
Host Name (7)	Host name of the issuing LAC or LNS
Vendor Name (8)	Vendor-specific LAC or LNS
Assigned Tunnel ID (9)	Assigns an ID to each tunnel on a multiplexed link of multiple tunnels between LAC and LNS
Receive Window Size (10)	Indicates the receiver's window size
Challenge (11)	Sender wishes to authenticate the tunnel
Challenge Response (13)	Peer responds to the Challenge message

Table 8–4   AVPs for call management

AVP Type (Value)	Function of AVP
Cause Code (12)	Provides information on a call disconnection
Assigned Session ID (14)	ID of the session over the tunnel
Call Serial Number (15)	Unique ID for a call for troubleshooting purposes
Minimum BPS (16)	Lowest acceptable line speed for the call, in bit/s
Maximum BPS (17)	Highest acceptable line speed for the call, in bit/s
Bearer Type (18)	Indicates bearer channel as analog or digital
Framing Type (19)	Indicates asynchronous or synchronous framing for call
Called Number (21)	Number to be called for an OCRQ, and called number for an ICRQ
Calling Number (22)	Originating number for incoming call
Sub-Address (23)	Additional dialing information
Tx Connect Speed (24)	Transmit speed of facility-(LAC) to remote system
Rx Connect Speed (38)	Receive speed of facility-remote system to LAC
Physical Channel ID (25)	L_1 channel ID (T1 trunk, E1 trunk, etc.)
Private Group ID (37)	Used by LAC to indicate a call associated with a customer group
Sequencing Required	Indicates sequencing must be supported on data channel

system. Most of the AVPs for Call Management deal with identifiers for the call, and the transmit/receive speeds between the LAC and the remote system.

In the event that the LAC answers a call and negotiates LCP with a remote system, the AVPs in Table 8–5 are used to authenticate the remote system, and confirm its identity. In addition, these AVPs are also used to provide configuration information about the remote system. This information allows the initiation of the LCP and authentication operations at the LNS, which would allow PPP to operate without renegotiation of LCP.

A few explanatory notes should prove to be helpful regarding some of the AVPs in Table 8–5. The authentication AVPs may be exchanged during a session establishment. This operation entails the forwarding of PPP authentication information obtained at the LAC and sent to the LNS for validation. As such, it means a new round of PPP authentication at these nodes, which may or may not entail a new round of LCP negotiations.

The Proxy Authen Type AVP (29) indicates what type of authentication is to be used. The supported types are: (0) for reserved; (1) textual user name and password; (2) PPP CHAP; (3) PPP PAP; (4) none; (5) Microsoft CHAP Version 1.

The Call Status AVPs are used by the LAC and LNS to send each other a variety of information (see Table 8–6). The Call Errors AVP defines the following fields:

Table 8–5 AVPs for LCP Negotiation and Authentication

AVP Type (Value)	Function of AVP
Initial Received LCP CONFREQ (26)	Provides LNS with initial the CONFREQ received at the LAC from the PPP peer
Last Send LCP CONFREQ (27)	Provides LNS with last CONFREQ sent by LAC to PPP peer
Last Received LCP CONFREQ (28)	Provides LNS with last CONFREQ received by LAC from PPP peer
Proxy Authen Type (29)	Determines if proxy authentication is to be used
Proxy Ajuthen Name (30)	Name of authenticating client
Proxy Authen Challenge (31)	The challenge sent by LAC to PPP peer
Proxy Authen ID (32)	Specifies ID value of the PPP authentication
Proxy Authen Response (33)	Specifies PPP authentication response received by LAC from PPP peer

Table 8–6   AVPs for Call Status

AVP Type (Value)	Function of AVP
Call Errors (34)	Used by LAC to send error information to LNS
ACCM (35)	Used by LNS to inform LAC of ACCM negotiated with PPP peer by the LNS

- *CRC Errors:* Number of PPP frames received with CRC errors since call was established.
- *Framing Errors:* Number of improperly framed PPP packets received.
- *Hardware Overruns:* Number of receive buffer overruns since call was established.
- *Buffer Overruns:* Number of buffer overruns detected since call was established.
- *Time-out Errors:* Number of time-outs since call was established.
- *Alignment Errors:* Number of alignment errors since call was established.

The ACCM AVP (35) is used to inform the LAC of the peer's asynchronous control character map (ACCM). It is used to enable or disable ASCII control character escapes (for the 32 control characters). This operation is described in RFC 1662, and earlier in this book.

The L2TP Control Messages

Before we examine some examples of L2TP tunnels, it is necessary to pause and review the major functions of the connection and control messages, those that are used to set up, maintain, and tear down the tunnel. Section 6 of [TOWN99] provides the detailed rules on the user of these messages, as well as the required and optional AVPs. This section is an overview of [TOWN99].

Table 8–7 lists the Control Connection Management and Call Management messages, and two other miscellaneous messages, as well as the number of each message type. You might find it helpful to refer to this table during this discussion, as well as the AVP tables just discussed.

Start-Control-Connection-Request (SCCRQ). The SCCRQ is used to initialize a tunnel between an LNS and an LAC. It is sent by either the LAC or the LNS to begin the tunnel establishment operations.

Table 8–7   The L2TP messages

Control Connection Management

0	(reserved)	
1	(SCCRQ)	Start-Control-Connection-Request
2	(SCCRP)	Start-Control-Connection-Reply
3	(SCCCN)	Start-Control-Connection-Connected
4	(StopCCN)	Stop-Control-Connection-Notification
5	(reserved)	
6	(HELLO)	Hello

Call Management

7	(OCRQ)	Outgoing-Call-Request
8	(OCRP)	Outgoing-Call-Reply
9	(OCCN)	Outgoing-Call-Connected
10	(ICRQ)	Incoming-Call-Request
11	(ICRP)	Incoming-Call-Reply
12	(ICCN)	Incoming-Call-Connected
13	(reserved)	
14	(CDN)	Call-Disconnect-Notify

Error Reporting

15	(WEN)	WAN-Error-Notify

PPP Session Control

16	(SLI)	Set-Link-Info

Note: 0, 5, and 13 are reserved for future use.

The following AVPs are present in the SCCRQ: (a) Message Type AVP, (b) Protocol Version, (c) Host Name, (d) Framing Capabilities, and (e) Assigned Tunnel ID. The Following AVPs are optional entries in SCCRQ: (a) Bearer Capabilities, (b) Receive Window Size, (c) Challenge, (d) Tie Breaker, (e) Firmware Revision, and (f) Vendor Name.

Start-Control-Connection-Reply (SCCRP). The SCCRP is sent in reply to a received SCCRQ message. SCCRP is used to indicate that the SCCRQ was accepted and establishment of the tunnel should continue.

The following AVPs are present in the SCCRP: (a) Message Type, (b) Protocol Version, (c) Framing Capabilities, (d) Host Name, (e) Assigned Tunnel ID. The following AVPs are optional entries: (a) Bearer Capabilities, (b) Firmware Revision, (c) Vendor Name, (d) Receive Window Size, (e) Challenge, and (f) Challenge Response.

Start-Control-Connection-Connected (SCCCN). The SCCCN is sent in reply to an SCCRP, and completes the tunnel establishment process. The following AVP is present in the SCCCN: (a) Message Type. The Challenge Response AVP is optional.

Stop-Control-Connection-Notification (StopCCN). The StopCCN is sent by either the LAC or LNS to inform its peer that the tunnel is being shut down and the control connection should be closed. In addition, all active sessions are implicitly cleared (without sending any explicit call control messages). There is no explicit reply to the message, only the implicit ACK that is received by the reliable control message transport layer.

The following AVPs are present in the StopCCN: (a) Message Type, (b) Assigned Tunnel ID, and (c) Result Code. There are no optional AVPs.

HELLO. This message is sent by either peer of a LAC-LNS control connection. This control message is used as a "keepalive" for the tunnel. The nature of how the Hello message is used is implementation-specific. The only AVP for this message is Message Type.

Outgoing-Call-Request (OCRQ). The OCRQ is sent by the LNS to the LAC to indicate that an outbound call from the LAC is to be established. It is the first in a three-message exchange used for establishing a session within the L2TP tunnel. It provides the LAC with information about the session, and about the call.

L2TP requires that an LNS must receive a Bearer Capabilities AVP during the tunnel establishment from an LAC in order to request an outgoing call to that LAC.

The following AVPs are present in the OCRQ: (a) Message Type, (b) Assigned Session ID, (c) Call Serial Number, (d) Minimum BPS, (e) Maximum BPS, (f) Bearer Type, (g) Framing Type, (h) Called Number. In addition the Sub-Address is an optional AVP.

Outgoing-Call-Reply (OCRP). The OCRP is sent by the LAC to the LNS in response to a received OCRQ message. It is the second in the three-message exchange used for establishing a session. It indicates that the LAC is able to attempt the outbound call, and it has AVPs that contain information about the call attempt.

The following AVPs are present in the OCRP: (a) Message Type, and (b) Assigned Session ID, while the Physical Channel ID is an option.

Outgoing-Call-Connected (OCCN). The OCCN is sent by the LAC to the LNS following the OCRP and after the outgoing call has been completed. It is the final message in a three-message exchange used for establishing a session, and is used to provide information about the requested outgoing call. It also contains information about the call, after it was established.

The following AVPs are present in the OCCN: (a) Message Type, (b) Tx Connect Speed, and (c) Framing Type. These AVPs are optional: (a) Rx Connect Speed, and (b) Sequencing Required.

Incoming-Call-Request (ICRQ). The ICRQ is sent by the LAC to the LNS when an incoming call is detected. It is the first in a three-message exchange used for establishing a session within the L2TP tunnel. ICRQ provides the LNS with parameter information for the session. [TOWN99] provides some useful guidance on the ICRQ procedure:

> The LAC may defer answering the call until it has received an ICRP from the LNS indicating that the session should be established. This mechanism allows the LNS to obtain sufficient information about the call before determining whether it should be answered or not. Alternatively, the LAC may answer the call, negotiate LCP and PPP authentication, and use the information gained to choose the LNS. In this case, the call has already been answered by the time the ICRP message is received; the LAC simply spoofs the "call indication" and "call answer" steps in this case.

The following AVPs are present in the ICRQ: (a) Message Type, (b) Assigned Session ID, and (c) Call Serial Number. The following AVPs are optional (a) Bearer Type, (b) Physical Channel ID, (c) Calling Number, (d) Called Number, and (e) Sub-Address.

Incoming-Call-Reply (ICRP). The ICRP is sent by the LNS to the LAC in response to a received ICRQ message. It is the second in the three-message exchange and indicates that the ICRQ message was acceptable, and to instruct the LAC to answer the call (if it had not already done so). It also allows the LNS to indicate necessary parameters for the L2TP session.

The following AVPs are in the ICRP: (a) Message Type, (b) Assigned Session ID. There are no optional AVPs.

Incoming-Call-Connected (ICCN). The ICCN is sent by the LAC to the LNS in response to a received ICRP message. It is the third message used for establishing sessions within the L2TP tunnel. The message indicates the ICRP message was accepted, and that the call has been answered. It also contains a parameter that gives more information about the answered call.

The following AVPs are present in the ICCN: (a) Message Type, (b) Tx Connect Speed, and (c) Framing Type. The following AVPs are optional: (a) Initial Received LCP CONFREQ, (b) Last Sent LCP CONFREQ, (c) Last Received LCP CONFREQ, (d) Proxy Authen Type (e) Proxy Authen Name, (f) Proxy Authen Challenge, (g) Proxy Authen ID,

(h) Proxy Authen Response, (I) Private Group ID, (j) Rx Connect Speed, and (k) Sequencing Required.

Call-Disconnect-Notify (CDN). The CDN is sent by either the LAC or LNS to request disconnection of a specific call within the tunnel. It informs the peer of the disconnection and the reason why the disconnection occurred. The peer then cleans up any resources, but does not send back any indication of success or failure for such cleanup.

The following AVPs are present in the CDN: (a) Message Type, (b) Result Code, and (c) Assigned Session ID, while the Q.932 Cause Code may be in the message as an option.

WAN-Error-Notify (WEN). This message is sent by the LAC to the LNS to indicate WAN error conditions (conditions that occur on the interface supporting PPP). The L2TP draft states that this message is sent only when an error occurs, and not more than once every sixty seconds. The notify counters are reset when a new call is established.

The following AVPs are present in the WEN: (a) Message Type, and (b) Call Errors. There are no optional AVPs.

Set-Link-Info (SLI). This message is sent by the LNS to the LAC to set PPP-negotiated options. These options can change at any time during the life of the call, and therefore the LAC must be able to update its internal call information and behavior on an active PPP session.

The following AVPs are present in the SLI: (a) Message Type, and (b) ACCM. There are no optional AVPs.

EXAMPLES OF L2TP OPERATIONS

We now piece together many of the concepts that have been explained in this chapter. Figure 8–6 will get us started. It shows how the L2TP peers communicate with each other for the establishment of a control connection, then a session. Remember that L2TP requires an initial connection to be brought up before the sessions can be set up. Also, recall that either the LAC or the LNS can set up the control connection.

Events 1–3 show the message exchange used for the initial control connection. The ZLB ACK in event 4 is sent if there are no more messages in the queue waiting to be sent to the peer. These messages can be sent and received by either the LAC or the LNS.

Remember that the SCCRQ must contain these AVPs: (a) Message Type AVP, (b) Protocol Version, (c) Host Name, (d) Framing Capabilities, and (e) Assigned Tunnel ID.

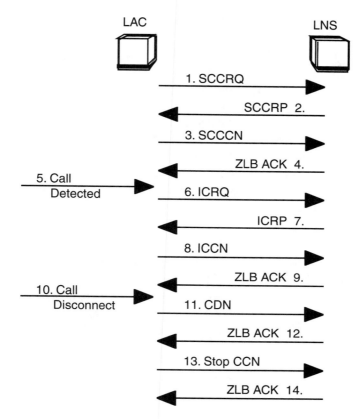

Figure 8–6   Example of the L2TP message exchange

The session set up is shown in events 5–9. It is unidirectional: (a) The LAC requests the LNS to accept a connection based on the LAC receiving an incoming call, and (b) the LNS requests the LAC to accept a session for an outgoing call. This example is an incoming call and in event 5, the call is detected. Each session corresponds to exactly one PPP stream.

Remember that the ICRQ message must contain these AVPs: (a) Message Type, (b) Assigned Session ID, and (c) Call Serial Number.

Events 10–12 show the session connection teardown, and events 13–14 show the control connection teardown, which is initiated in event 10 with a user call disconnect signal. Control connection teardown can be initiated by either the LAC or the LNS.

WINDOW MANAGEMENT AND ACCOUNTING FOR TRAFFIC

The L2TP methods for window management and accounting for traffic are similar to PPP's LAPB option discussed in Chapter 6. The Ns and Nr fields in the L2TP message header (see Figure 8–4) perform the same functions as the LAPB N(S) and N(R) fields. Some aspects of this part of L2TP also resemble TCP operations.

Messages are allowed to arrive out-of-order. They can be queued for later in-order delivery, or they may be discarded, depending on the implementation. Message retransmissions use an exponential back-off interval. Each retransmission wait is twice the time interval as the previous transmission.

Slow Start

For resending control messages, L2TP recommends an approach used in some TCP implementations called slow start and congestion avoidance. Figure 8–7 shows an example of the slow start.

Slow start uses a variable called the congestion window (*cwnd*). The sending L2TP module is allowed to increment *cwnd* when it receives acknowledgments of previously transmitted messages.

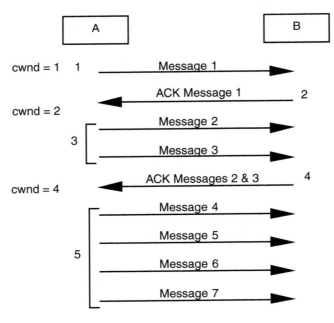

Figure 8–7   The slow start

Upon initialization, L2TP A sends one message; at this time *cwnd* = 1. In event 2, L2TP B acknowledges TCP A's message 1 which allows L2TP A to increment *cwnd* = 2. In event 3, it sends two messages numbered 2 and 3.

Notice that slow start is really not a slow start but an exponential start. In event 4, L2TP B acknowledges segments 2 and 3 which allows L2TP A to increment *cwnd* to a value of 4, and it then sends the four messages shown in event 5.

This exponential increase in the transmission of messages from L2TP A is constrained by its transmit window, which of course is governed by L2TP B.

One point is noteworthy here. The variable *cwnd* will not continue to be increased exponentially if a time-out occurs. Then, the L2TP sending module must resend those messages. In this situation, *cwnd* is set to one message, which is in harmony with the slow start concept: take it easy and don't send traffic if the network is congested.

Congestion Avoidance

The sending L2TP module will not send traffic continuously at an exponential rate if the ACKs to the messages are delayed. In essence, a point is reached where the sending L2TP backs-off its sending of messages (see Figure 8–8).

Two variables are pertinent here: (a) *cwnd* and (b) *ssthresh*. The operation proceeds as follows. If the L2TP module detects congestion either through a time-out or through the reception of duplicate acknowledgments, a value is saved in *ssthresh*. This value must be one-half of the

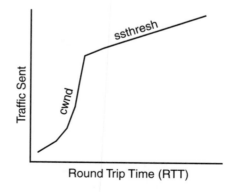

Figure 8–8   Using the ssthresh variable

current window size, but can be at least two messages. Moreover, if a time-out occurs, *cwnd* is reset to the value of 1 which reinitializes the slow-start operation.

Therefore, congestion avoidance requires that *cwnd* must be incremented by 1/*cwnd* each time an ACK is received. Consequently, for this situation, the result is a linear increase in the traffic sent.

Congestion avoidance actually goes one step further, in addition to *cwnd* being increased by 1/*cwnd*, it has another factor added which is the message size/8. The concept of using message size/8 is to allow the faster opening of windows for sessions that were initialized with large windows.

SECURITY CONSIDERATIONS

Chapter 5 explains the major security aspects of PPP. L2TP defines its security procedures in Section 9.0 of [TOWN99], and this part of the chapter is a summary of Section 9.0.

Tunnel Endpoint Security

The tunnel endpoints may perform (as on option) an authentication procedure with one another during tunnel establishment. This authentication has the same security attributes as CHAP, and has protection against replay and snooping during the tunnel establishment process, but it is not designed to provide any authentication beyond the tunnel establishment. The authentication procedure requires that the LAC and LNS share a single secret, both as the challenging party and the challenged party.

Since a single secret is used, the tunnel authentication AVPs include differentiating values in the CHAP ID fields for each message digest calculation to guard against replay attacks.

If security support is provided, L2TP requires that encryption, integrity and authentication services be provided. L2TP is only concerned with confidentiality, authenticity, and integrity of the L2TP packets between its tunnel endpoints (the LAC and LNS).

L2TP and IPSec

IPSec provides packet-level security via the ESP and/or AH. IPSec defines access-control features that are required of a compliant IPSec implementation. These features allow filtering of packets based upon network and transport layer characteristics such as IP address, ports, etc. In

L2TP, analogous filtering is performed at the PPP layer or network layer above L2TP. These network layer access control features may be handled at the LNS via vendor-specific authorization features based upon the authenticated PPP user, or at the network layer itself by using IPSec transport mode end-to-end between the communicating hosts.

EXTENSIONS

Since the Message Type AVP found first in a control message must have the M bit set, an L2TP implementation cannot safely send a control message without first determining that the peer will understand the message. A signaling mechanism must therefore be defined which allows this information to be known.

[SHEA98][2] specifies the use of a new AVP called the Extensions AVP that can be sent in the SCCRQ and SCCRP control messages. The purpose of this new AVP is to signal to the peer the extensions supported by the sending implementation.

The Extensions AVP encodes the L2TP extensions supported by the sending implementation. This AVP is not marked as mandatory. The AVP itself is optional in the SCCRQ and SCCRP control messages.

LINK EXTENSIONS

The separation of the LAC and LNS across multiple links with L2TP and logical separation of the responsibilities of each with respect to negotiated link parameters translates into a lack of awareness between the tunnel endpoints. Examples of these link parameters are the size of the FCS field, use of AHDLC, size of the I field, etc.

When possible, Proxy LCP provides a mechanism to negotiate link parameters at the LAC and communicate these values to the LNS. However, there are instances where negotiation of LCP must take place at the LNS. Therefore, some direction by the LAC as to what parameters are acceptable, as well as some communication from the LNS as to what parameters have been negotiated, is desirable.

---

[2][SHEA98]Shea, Richard. "Framework for L2TP Message Extensions", draft-ietf-pppext-l2tpmsgext-00.txt, November 1998.

[TOWN98][3] defines the AVPs to allow the LAC and the LNS to communicate complete LCP information in order to react accordingly. LCP option information is structured in the same way as the Proxy LCP AVPs are in the L2TP specification discussed earlier in this chapter. The operation involves the encapsulation of a PPP LCP Configure-Request or Configure-ACK packet within an L2TP AVP. I refer you to [TOWN98] if you need more information on this topic.

SUMMARY

L2TP allows the use of the PPP procedures between different networks and across multiple communications links. With L2TP, PPP is extended as an encapsulation and negotiation protocol to allow the transport of PPP and user traffic between different networks and nodes.

L2TP's importance can be seen by a wide variety of AVPs and Internet standards that define its relationship to other systems and protocols. It is a valuable tool to a network manager, simply because it allows an enterprise to further exploit the PPP services.

---

[3][TOWN98] Townsley, Mark W. L2TP Link Extensions, draft-ietf-ppext-12tp-link-oo.txt, November, 1998.

9

L2TP and Other Protocols and Services

L2TP might operate over different kinds of networks, and with different types of protocols. As this protocol finds its way into internets, its operations will impinge on other systems and networks, such as ATM, and Frame Relay. It will surely have an impact in cellular mobile networks wherein IP users are roaming about, and still need PPP services. This chapter examines these "other systems," and explains how L2TP interworks with them.

RUNNING L2TP OVER ATM OR FRAME RELAY

Since many backbone networks are using ATM or Frame Relay technologies (See Figure 9–1), it makes sense to define a method of encapsulating L2TP over these bearer services. Currently, the following Internet drafts are being developed to set standards for these operations. [DAVI99][1] defines the operations of L2TP over ATM. [T'JO99][2] defines

---

[1][DAVI99] Davison, Mike, Lin, Arthur, Sin gh, Ajoy, Stephens, John, Turner, Rollins, Senthilnathan, J. "L2TP Over AAL5 and FUNI," draft-ietf-ppext-12tp-atm-02.txt, April, 1999.

[2][T'JO99] T'Joens, Yves, Crivellari, Paolo, Hermans, Laurent, "Layer Two Tunnelling Protocol: ATM Access Network Extensions," draft-ietf-ppext-12tp-atmext-00.txt, January, 1999.

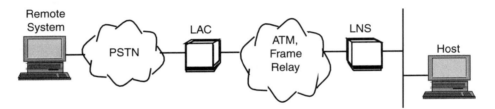

Figure 9–1   Running L2TP over ATM or Frame Relay

ATM access extensions for L2TP. The third draft of interest in this section is [RAWA98],[3] which describes the rules for running L2TP over Frame Relay.

Review of ATM and Frame Relay Encapsulation Procedures

The term encapsulation refers to an operation in which a transport network, such as PPP, L2TP, ATM, or Frame Relay, carries Protocol Data Units (PDUs) from other protocols through the transport network. These other encapsulated protocols could be IP, AppleTalk, SNA, DECnet, etc. that operate at the upper layers of the OSI layered model, typically at layer 3 and above. The transport network performs lower layer bearer services, typically at layers 1 and 2, and perhaps layer 3 of the model.

We have discussed in several parts of this book the encapsulation operations of PPP and L2TP. However, PPP and L2TP are not transport systems; they operate over ATM and Frame Relay networks. Therefore, in most internets, multiple encapsulations occur: L2TP is encapsulated into UDP, which is encapsulated into IP, which is encapsulated into (say) ATM, which is encapsulated into (say) SONET.

To invoke encapsulation operations, the user must furnish the network with a specific identifier to distinguish the type of traffic that is to be sent through the transport network. This identifier is important, because the network and the receiving user machine must invoke support procedures that apply to the specific type of traffic; that is, a specific protocol family, such as X.25, IP, SNA, etc. After all, a node, such as a router, cannot process the traffic until it knows about the type of traffic, such as its header contents and the syntax of the traffic, which vary depending on the protocol.

---

[3][RAWA98]. Rawat, Vipin, Tio, Rene, "Layer Two Tunneling Protocol (L2TP) over Frame Relay," draft-ietf-pppext-12tp-fr-01.txt, December, 1998.

The concepts of encapsulation are relatively straightforward. Unfortunately, more than one encapsulation procedure is used by ATM and Frame Relay, which complicates the issue. To muddy the waters even more, ATM and Frame Relay use more than one encapsulation field as part of these operations. Those fields (and encapsulation standards) that are relevant to this discussion are:[4]

Control	The control field, as established in High-Level Data Link Control (HDLC) standards
NLPID	The network level protocol ID, as established in the ISO/IEC TR 9577 standard
PID	Protocol ID, as established in RFCs 826 and 1042
OUI	The organization unique id, as established in RFCs 826 and 1042
SNAP	Subnetwork Access Protocol, which defines the OUI and PID
LLC	The logical link control protocol, as established in the IEEE 802.1a standards

ATM and L2TP

The encapsulation of L2TP over ATM permits two types of encapsulation: (a) LLC, and (b) virtual circuit multiplexing. Figure 9–2 shows the format for these two types.

Figure 9–2(a) shows the LLC type. The fields are set to the following values. The IEEE 802.2 LLC header contains the source and destination service access point (SAP) of xAA, followed by a frame type of unnumbered Information (value x03). This LLC header indicates that an IEEE 802.1a SNAP header follows. The SNAP header contains the three octet Organizational Unique Identifier (OUI) value of x00-00-5E which identifies IANA (Internet Assigned Numbers Authority.) The two octet Protocol Identifier (PID) identifies L2TP as the encapsulated protocol (x0007). The PID value is determined by IANA.

Figure 9–2(b) shows the virtual circuit multiplexing type. This method of running L2TP over AAL5 is an alternative technique to LLC encapsulated L2TP over AAL5 when both LAC and LNS use AAL5 as op-

---

[4]I refer you to a detailed discussion encapsulation operations contained in a companion book to this series, titled, *ATM Vol III: Internetworking with ATM,* by Uyless Black, Prentice Hall, 1998.

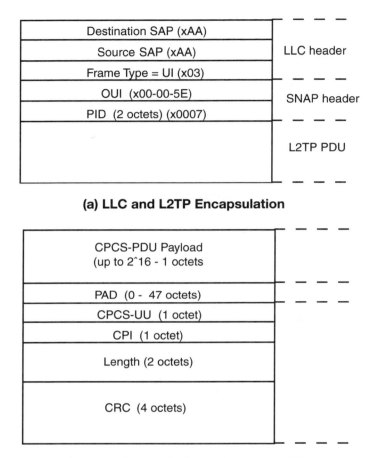

(a) LLC and L2TP Encapsulation

(b) Virtual Circuit Multiplexing and L2TP

Figure 9–2   L2TP over ATM encapsulation types

posed to the Frame UNI (FUNI). FUNI is a method to send simple L_2 frames (non-ATM cells) to and from an ATM node and a user node. In this case the L2TP PDU is the AAL5 payload.

The PAD field pads the CPCS-PDU to fit exactly into the ATM cell. The CPCS-UU (User-to-User indication) field is used to transparently transfer user to user information. The CPI (Common Part Indicator) field aligns the CPCS-PDU trailer to 64 bits. The Length field indicates the length, in octets, of the payload. The CRC field is computed over the entire CPCS-PDU except the CRC field itself.

QOS Support. [DAVI99] defines these operations to support the client's quality of service needs. In order to provide a required QOS to the client (and possibly different quality of service levels to different client connections), there may be more than one AAL5 connection between the LAC and the LNS.

A tunnel is initially created over an AAL5 connection. A subsequent ATM call (the ATM connection setup operation) to the LAC may require that the LAC open a new AAL5 connection to satisfy QOS requirements of that call. If an implementation determines that multiple tunnels are required to a given peer, each tunnel is based on a separate AAL5 connection.

Frame Relay and L2TP

Figure 9–3 shows the Frame Relay frame used to encapsulate L2TP. The frame format for L2TP is based on the ISO NLPID, and then SNAP encapsulation. This format uses ISO NLPID value followed by Organizational Unique Identifier and a PID. The NLPID is set to x80, reserved for the identification of the SNAP header.

The SNAP header contains the three octet Organizational Unique Identifier (OUI) value of x00-00-5E identifies IANA (Internet Assigned Numbers Authority.) The two octet Protocol Identifier (PID) identifies L2TP as the encapsulated protocol (x0007). The PID value is determined by IANA.

QOS Support. [RAWA98] defines no operations to support the client's QOS requirements. They are left to individual implementations.

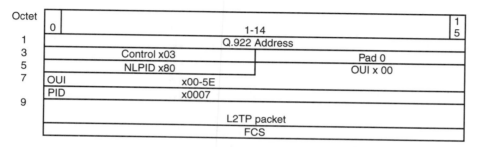

Figure 9–3   Frame Relay and L2TP

L2TP-OVER-IP MTU PATH DISCOVERY (L2TPMTU)

This section covers L2TP over IP. The problems encountered with fragmentation are examined, as well as the process of path discovery to support a maximum transmission unit (MTU) size.

Review of IP Fragmentation

The IP protocol uses three fields in the header to control datagram fragmentation and reassembly. These fields are the *identifier*, *flags*, and *fragmentation offset*. The identifier field is used to uniquely identify all fragments from an original datagram. It is used with the source address at the receiving host to identify the fragment.

The flags field contains bits to determine if the datagram may be fragmented. If fragmented, one of the bits can be set to determine if this fragment is the last fragment of the datagram. The bit that allows or disallows fragmentation is called the "Don't Fragment" (DF) bit.

The fragmentation offset field contains a value which specifies the relative position of the fragment to the original datagram. The value is initialized as 0 and is subsequently set to the proper number if/when an IP node fragments the data. The value is measured in units of eight bytes.

An IP datagram may traverse a number of different networks that use different datagram sizes on their links, and all networks have a maximum size, called the maximum transmission unit (MTU). Therefore, IP contains procedures for dividing (fragmenting) a large datagram into smaller datagrams. It also allows the user application to stipulate that fragmentation may or may not occur. Of course, it must also use a reassembly mechanism at the final destination which places the fragments back into the order originally transmitted.

When an IP gateway node receives a datagram which is too big to be transmitted by the transit subnetwork, it uses its fragmentation operations. It divides the datagram into two or more pieces (with alignment on 8-octet boundaries). Each of the fragmented pieces has a header attached containing identification, addressing, and as another option, all options pertaining to the original datagram. The fragmented packets also have information attached to them defining the position of the fragment within the original datagram, as well as an indication if this fragment is the last fragment. The flags (the 3 bits) are used as follows:

- *Bit 0* = reserved
- *Bit 1;* 0 = fragmentation and 1 = don't fragment
- *Bit 2 (M bit)*; 0 = last fragment and 1 = more fragments

Interestingly, IP handles each fragment operation independently. That is to say, the fragments may traverse different paths to the intended destination, and they may be subject to further fragmentation if they pass through links and networks that use smaller data units. The next node uses the offset value in the incoming fragment to determine the offset values of fragmented datagrams. If further fragmentation is done at another node, the fragment offset value is set to the location that this fragment fits relative to the original datagram and not the preceding fragmented packet.

The Problem and Solution

The problem with all these operations is that they entail a considerable amount of processing at each node performing the fragmentation operations. In some situations, fragmentation can adversely affect the performance of a network. Yet if the links on the path from a sender to a receiver are configured with an MTU that is smaller than the transmitted datagram, either the traffic is fragmented or it is discarded.

To solve this problem, most systems today employ MTU path discovery. This operation uses a ping protocol to send IP datagrams into an internet with the don't fragment flag set to 1. If the IP datagram encounters a link whose MTU is smaller than the datagram, the datagram is discarded and an ICMP diagnostic message is returned to the originator, indicating that fragmentation is needed on this path. Eventually, the ping operation may reveal a path on which fragmentation is not needed.

Problem with MTU Path Discovery on L2TP Tunnels

If L2TP is run over IP, fragmentation of the tunneled IP datagrams may occur due to different path MTU values between the L2TP peers. One might think, "Fine, let's just run MTU path discovery through the tunnel, and that solves the problem." Not quite. The reason is that conventional MTU path discovery may entail the resending of a packet many times, and L2TP tears down a tunnel if it detects this situation. Therefore this rather simple problem requires a different approach.

L2TPMTU Operations

To solve this problem, [SHEA98][5] has proposed an approach where MTU path discovery across a L2TP tunnel is performed through a separate L2TP channel, called the discovery channel. This channel is used to send messages between L2TP peers (an LAC and an LNS) in order to discover a path MTU. The remainder of this section of the book provides an overview of this draft.

While L2TPMTU is rather elaborate, its basic design concept is quite straightforward. If an IP datagram is being tunneled with the DF bit set and the sending L2TP endpoint knows that the resulting L2TP-encapsulated packet would be IP fragmented, the L2TP endpoint sends an ICMP message to the sending IP host specifying an adjusted MTU at which L2TP-encapsulated packets will not be fragmented.

If an IP datagram is being tunneled with the DF bit set in its header and it does not meet the above condition, the DF bit is set in the L2TP data channel packet.

Two new control channel messages are used for path MTU discovery. They are used if the peers indicate they support L2TPMTU. The first message is LRPMTU-Request (LRPMTURQ). This message is sent to the peer to indicate the value of the path MTU. The peer that receives this message simply responds with the LRPMTU-Reply (LRPMTURP).

The channel discovery messages are exchanged between L2TP peers in order to inform peers about their capability to support L2TPMTU operations. The manner in which these messages are invoked and the manner in which they are acted upon is subject to several rules on how the L2TP peer can process IP-in-PPP packets. We must leave these details to your further investigations into the IETF draft.

MOBILE PPP (MPPP)

Mobile PPP (MPPP) is used with L2TP and is documented in [CHUA99].[6] It is possible for a mobile user's LAC to change during a PPP session. For example, a foreign service provider to which the mobile user has roamed may be different from the user's home service provider.

---

[5][SHEA98] Shea, Richard. "L2TP-over-IP Path MTU Discovery (L2TPMTU)." Draft-ietf-pppext-12tpmut-00.txt, January, 1998.

[6][CHUA99] Chuah, M. C., Grosser, D., Rai, G., Teplitsky, Jacob. "Mobile PPP (MPPP)," draft-ietf-pppext-mppp-00.txt.

MPPP allows for a change of LACs during the lifetime of a PPP session without incurring the delay and overhead of setting up a new PPP session. [CHUA99] presents different methods of supporting this feature, and they are summarized in this section.

As shown in Figure 9–4, mobile nodes (MN) can dial up a PPP server to access the internet. A link level tunnel is created between the mobile node's serving interworking function (IWF) and the PPP server. If the mobile node moves to another IWF, the tunnel between the old IWF is torn down and a new tunnel to the new IWF is created.

We learned in Chapter 5 that the PPP server authenticates the mobile nodes using a PPP authentication protocol, such as CHAP. Since the server is not aware of mobile node handovers in a wireless network, it does not perform any authentication when a mobile node changes its serving IWF. Also, under existing standards, the user is not allowed to change its NAS during a PPP session. Of course in the mobile environment, a mobile node may traverse into a serving area that has a different NAS.

MPPP adds a mobile feature to the L2TP to provide wide area mobility to nodes without having to renegotiate the PPP session during a handoff. If the mobile node is running the IP/PPP protocol stack, no changes are needed at the mobile node, because the actions entail the old NAS/LAC, transferring the PPP session to the new NAS/LAC.

The Three Methods

The three methods for implementing MPPP are listed below. It should be stated that the authors of MPPP prefer CTA because it provides end-to-end flow control for the PPP session, and it requires less CPU processing than ITA. Furthermore, CTA requires software changes only to LAC, whereas the other two require changes to both nodes.

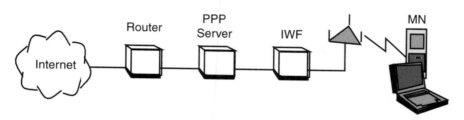

Figure 9–4   Typical PPP and mobile node setup

- Simple AVP Approach (SAA)
- Independent Tunnel Approach (ITA)
- Concatenated Tunnel Approach (CTA)

Simple AVP Approach (SAA). Figure 9–5 shows the message exchange between the affected nodes to support SAA. The messages shown in this figure are explained Chapter 8, so we will not dwell on them here, but will confine ourselves to the specifics of this operation.

The operation requires that a link-layer message received at the new LAC include information that allows the new LAC (with a local server) to determine which LNS the new LAC is to communicate with (event 1). During the L2TP tunnel set-up between the new LAC and the LNS, the LNS responds with a Mobile AVP in its SCCRP message, which means it supports the mobility feature (events 2 and 3). The LNS receives the SCCCN message and the ICRQ message with an attached User AVP (events 4 and 5). This information is interpreted as a possible signal of a handoff for an existing PPP call. Using the information provided in the User AVP, the LNS uses its local server to identity the mobile node's old LAC.

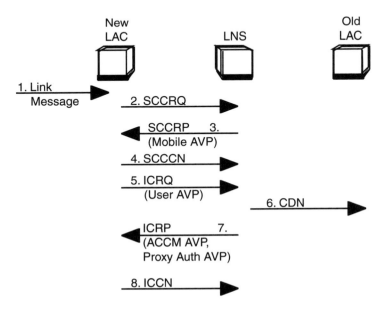

Figure 9–5   The simple AVP approach (SAA)

If the LNS cannot accept the call handoff (not shown in this example), the LNS sends a CDN message to the new LAC. In this example, the LNS accepts the handoff, by sending the CDN message to the old LAC (event 6). The LNS then replies with an ICRP message to the new LAC (event 7) with the ACCN AUP and proxy authenticate AUP, and an ICCN message is returned in event 8.

SAA is a simple operation, but it may take a while to put into effect because the new LAC and the LNS may be in a remote system. In addition, SAA makes no assumption about security operations, so there must be additional agreements about how to authenticate the new LAC.

Concatenated Tunnel Approach (CTA). The CTA approach is shown in Figure 9–6. Here, there is one L2TP session per call. The L2TP session spans two hops: (a) one between the serving LAC and the anchor LAC, (b) the other between the anchor LAC and the LNS. As you can see,

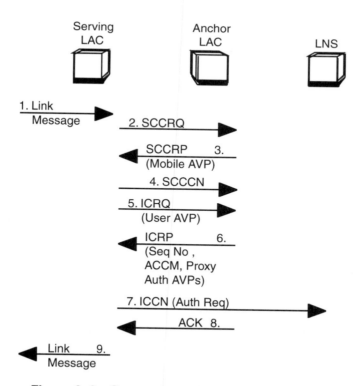

Figure 9–6   Concatenated Tunnel Approach (CTA)

the CTA message flow is similar to that of ITA. Since there is only one flow control procedure on the two-hop session, the anchor LAC sends a sequence number AVP (Nr, Ns) to the serving LAC so this node knows what sequence numbers with which to begin its operations. The job of the anchor LAC is relatively simple; its main job is to update the Nr and Ns values in the messages as they flow through the anchor LAC. But, unlike the ITA approach, this node does not have to participate in the flow control operations on these sessions.

IPSec AND L2TP

IPSec was introduced in Chapter 5, and this section assumes you have read this material. Recall that IPSec defines the protocols used in implementing the security association in an internet. The authoritative source for IPSec and L2TP operations is [PATE99].[7] This section provides a summary of [PATE99] and uses the term the L2TP security protocol to mean the joint operations of IPSec and L2TP.

Unto themselves, L2TP and PPP authentication and encryption do not meet the security requirements for L2TP. L2TP tunnel set-ups typically include authentication between the LAC and LNS, but the control and data packets are not protected. PPP encryption meets confidentiality requirements for PPP traffic but does not address authentication, integrity and key management requirements. So PPP encryption is a weak security service.

To address these threats, the L2TP security protocol provides authentication, integrity, and replay protection for control packets, and it may provide confidentiality of control packets. It provides integrity and replay protection of data packets, and it may provide confidentiality of data packets. To fulfill these obligations, the L2TP security protocol is organized around two types of tunnels: (a) the compulsory tunnel and (b) the voluntary tunnel.

The Compulsory Tunnel

The compulsory tunnel requires no action from the user, and the user has no choice in the matter. The tunnel is created by the LAC and the LNS, with the user simply dialing into the LAC. The LAC sends the

---

[7][PATE99] Patel, Baiju and Aboba, Bernard. "Securing L2TP Using IPSec," draft-ietf-ppext-12tp-security-03.txt, 2 Februay 1999.

PPP traffic to the LNS, which is first encapsulated into L2TP, second it is encapsulated into IP, and third it is encapsulated into IPSec. The IPSec header reveals the Security Association between the LAC and LNS, and therefore the LNS will know the appropriate security services that are associated with the incoming packet.

Since the end user of this PPP session may request PPP-based security measures (such as confidentiality), the LAC must be capable of negotiating the IP secure tunnel with the LNS such that IPSec operations do not duplicate those of PPP. As an example, IPSec ESP with null encryption may be requested by the LAC, and the LNS may request replay protection.

If the dial-in user knows that IPSec tunnels are available, the user may choose not to request PPP security services, and leave it to the IPSec tunnel to provide them.

The Voluntary Tunnel

The voluntary tunnel requires that a tunnel must be created by the user. In this situation, the LAC is on the same machine as the user. The NAS simply sends the L2TP packets to/from the LAC/LNS; the NAS does not have to support L2TP.

The dial-in user has knowledge of PPP authentication as well as IPSec Security Association. Likewise, the LNS knows about the Security Association. The dial-in user and LNS should be able to avoid use of PPP encryption and compression. They can negotiate IPSec confidentiality, authentication, and Integrity support services instead.

Summary of L2TP Requirements for Security

Given the use of voluntary or compulsory tunnels, the L2TP requirements for security (the L2TP security protocol) may be summarized as follows:

- Must provide authentication, integrity and replay protection for L2TP control packets.
- Should protect confidentiality of control packets.
- Must provide integrity and replay protection of data packets.
- May protect confidentiality of data packets.
- Must provide a scalable approach to key management.
- Must implement IPSec ESP for L2TP control packets.
- Should implement IPSec ESP for L2TP data packets.

- Must implement anti-replay mechanisms for IPSec.
- Must meet key management operations of IPSec and its key management requirements (the Internet key management protocols).

RADIUS AND L2TP

Chapter 5 is devoted to PPP and security operations, and provides an explanation of RADIUS. This discussion assumes you have read about RADIUS. This section summarizes the Internet draft from the RADIUS Working Group [ABOD98].[8]

Before we began this analysis, some additional RADIUS definitions are needed, as they pertain to L2TP. In addition, the voluntary and compulsory tunneling definitions, described earlier in this chapter, still hold for this discussion.

- *Tunnel Network Server:* This device terminates a tunnel, and is at the LNS.
- *RADIUS authentication server:* This server provides for authentication/authorization.
- *RADIUS proxy:* To the L2TP NAS, the RADIUS proxy appears as a RADIUS server, and to the RADIUS server, the proxy appears as a RADIUS client.

Other Types of Tunnels

Two other types of tunnels are described in these operations. The static tunnel has all users tunneled to a specific endpoint. The realm-tunnel has the tunnel endpoint determined by a user ID. The static tunnel requires a dedicated NAS, and the realm-tunnel treats all users within the realm the same way.

Authentication Alternatives

Two authentication alternatives are defined in [ABOD98]. They are single authentication and dual authentication. With single authentica-

---

[8][ABOD98] Aboda, Bernard and Zorn, Geln, "Implementation of L2TP Compulsory Tunneling via RADIUS," draft-ietf-radius-tunnel-imp-04.txt, 9 October 1998.

tion, the user is authenticated at the NAS *or* the tunnel server. With dual authentication, the user is authenticated at the NAS *and* the tunnel server. This section describes these two alternatives in more detail.

Single Authentication. Single authentication alternatives include three approaches. The first approach is NAS authentication, and entails all the authentication and tunneling operations occurring at the NAS. The second approach is NAS authentication and RADIUS reply forwarding, and entails authentication and authorization occurring once at the NAS with the RADIUS reply forwarded to the tunnel server.[9] The third approach is the tunnel server authentication, with authentication and authorization occurring once at the tunnel server. There are many rules and advantages/disadvantages pertaining to these approaches, and I leave you to [ABOD98] for these details.

First, we take a look at NAS authentication. Its attraction is that all accounting is performed at the NAS, and the operations are performed only once, but there is no authentication with the tunnel server; therefore, the tunnel server must trust the NAS.

NAS authentication is employed along with LCP forwarding and tunnel authentication, both of which are supported in L2TP. The tunnel server can be set up to accept all calls occurring within authenticated tunnels, without requiring PPP authentication. Figure 9–7 shows how the NAS authentication operations occur.

In event 1, an incoming call is placed to the NAS, then LCP negotiation begins, followed by PPP authentication. To authenticate the client, the NAS sends a RADIUS Access-Request packet to the RADIUS server, shown in event 2. In event 3, the RADIUS server returns an Access-Accept (or an Access-Reject, not shown here).

If an L2TP tunnel is indicated (which is the case here), the NAS and tunnel server bring up the L2TP tunnel, as shown in events 4, 5, and 6. In this example, the NAS employs LCP forwarding, but it is permitted for the tunnel server to renegotiate LCP. If LCP is negotiated, the NAS must send an LCP Configure-Request packet to start this process.

---

[9]The authors of this draft do not recommend this alternative for the following reason. If the reply comes directly from a RADIUS server, it would become unmanageable if a RADIUS proxy is involved, since the reply would be authenticated using the secret shared by the client and proxy, rather than the RADIUS server. The reason is that the server shares secrets with all NASs.

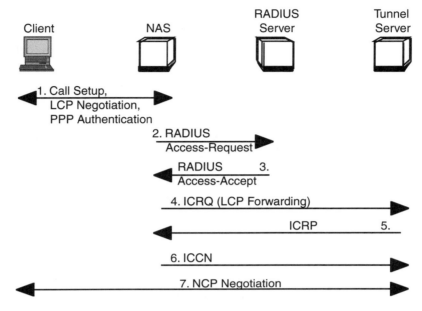

Figure 9–7   NAS authentication

In event 7, the client starts the NCP negotiation with the tunnel server. Notice that the NAS is not involved with the NCP negotiation because address assignments are performed at the tunnel server.

The third approach for single authentication is tunnel-server authentication. As stated earlier, the tunnel-server provides authentication and authorization (and it is performed once). The NAS determines that the user is to be tunneled through either a RADIUS or NAS configuration. For the RADIUS configuration, the determination is made though one of these methods: (a) telephone-number based authentication, or (b) UserID. With the first method, the RADIUS server can use the calling party phone number to authorize the users, or use other fields in the packet to provide tunnel attributes (calling or called-station IDs). With the first method, a phone number for the ID is replaced by the RADIUS userID. Once again, there are a variety of rules on how these identifiers are used; for this discussion, we will use an example based on using the telephone number. Figure 9–8 shows the packet flow for this operation.

The packet flow is similar to the previous example of NAS authentication. The major difference is that the NAS does not begin LCP negotiation and PPP authentication until the tunnel is set up. As a consequence, LCP need not be negotiated between the client and the tunnel server. In addition, LCP forwarding is not invoked. As shown in event 11, the client

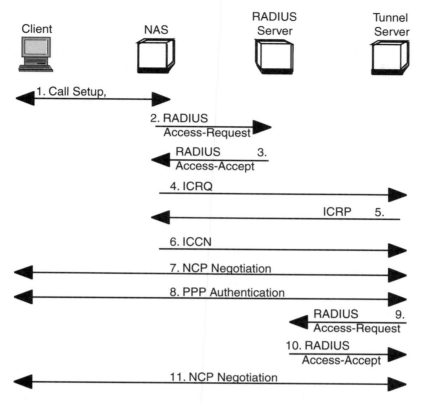

Figure 9–8   Telephone-Number-Based Authentication

and tunnel server proceed directly to NCP negotiation. Also, the RADIUS packet exchange in events 9 and 10 between the two servers is optional.

A few more points should be helpful in understanding this operation. The RADIUS-Access/-Accept contains sufficient information to bring up a control connection, which is accomplished by the L2TP packet exchange in events 4, 5, and 6. The L2TP message to the tunnel server contains sufficient information to uniquely identify the call. After these operations, data can now be transported through the tunnel.

MULTIPROTOCOL LABEL-SWITCHING (MPLS) EXTENSION

Label switching is a catchall term that encompasses a wide range of relaying techniques. Other terms used are swapping and mapping. But whatever the term or technique employed, label switching entails using a value that is associated with (and part of the header of) a packet. It is not an address; it does not have any topological or geographical significance. It is simply a number that is reserved to identify a specific flow of packets from a sender to a receiver, or receivers. MPLS provides a standard for the distribution of routing labels between neighbor LSRs.

[CALH99][10] describes an L2TP extension that two L2TP peers can negotiate the use of an MPLS label (Mlabel) for an L2TP session. The procedure provides either the LNS or LAC with an Mlabel with which to initiate the creation of an MPLS path to the peer. In addition, each session within the tunnel can have its own label.

[CALH99] does not define how the label is advertised and distributed, which is left to the Label Distribution Protocol. It assumes OSPF or BGP has made the necessary route discovery, and a label is associated with the appropriate addresses.

The procedure assumes that the tunnel initiator determines what the user's appropriate label is and sends the value in either the ICRQ or OCRQ messages. The tunnel terminator can respond to the message by stating what it believes is the user's appropriate label.

Other Drafts of Interest

Here are some other works-in-progress drafts that you might find useful in your work.

Alternate Data Channel Extension

Under certain conditions, it may be desirable to send user traffic (the data portion of the L2TP tunnel) over a different media than the control traffic. The precedent for this approach is the tried-and-true out-of-band signaling systems that have demonstrated that it can be more efficient to use a separate physical media for signaling (control) traffic. SS7 is one example of this approach. Eventually, L2TP might need this set-up as well, so [PALT97][11] defines a procedure and an AVP to meet this requirement.

L2TP Dynamic Data Window Adjustment

Some of the functions of L2TP resemble those of the layer-4 protocol TCP. Sequencing, time-outs, and flow control mechanisms are all part of

---

[10][CALH99]. Calhoun, Pat R, Pierce, Ken. "L2TP Multi-protocol Label Switching Extension," draft-ietf-pppext-12tp-mple-02.txt, February, 1999.

[11][PALT97] Palter, William. "L2TP Alternate Data Channel (L2TPADC)," draft-ietf-pppext-12tpadc-00.txt, January, 1997.

the TCP procedures. That is one reason L2TP runs on top of UDP, which does not provide these functions. To meet the needs of flexible flow-control operations across the L2TP tunnel, [SHEA98a][12] describes a method to implement a dynamic window adjustment procedure for data sessions.

IP Tunnel MIB

Finally, for those readers who are implementing or managing an L2TP system, the IP Tunnel MIB specification is an important tool. As with all the Internet MIBs, this MIB defines the most important objects pertaining to L2TP. The IP Tunnel MIB contains two tables: (a) the Tunnel Interface Table contains information on the tunnels known to a node, and (b) the Tunnel Configuration Table, contains information used to create tunnels, as well as information on mapping endpoint addresses to MIB interface index values. This draft is available in [THAL99].[13]

SUMMARY

Due to the importance of L2TP in supporting PPP operations, the protocol might operate over different kinds of networks, and with different types of protocols. With its growing use, it is quite likely that L2TP will become a pervasive protocol. Therefore, the Internet Working Groups are in the process of defining the specifications that will permit L2TP to operate gracefully with other systems and protocols. This chapter has provided an overview of them.

---

[12][SHEA98a]. Shea, Richard. "L2TP Dynamic Data Window Adjustment." Draft-ietf-ppext-12tpdwin-01.txt, November, 1998.

[13][THAL99]. Thaler, Dave. "IP Tunnel MIB," draft-ietf-ifmib-tunnel-mib-03.txt, April, 1999.

Appendix A

HDLC Overview

Since PPP operates as a link-layer protocol, and since it uses many of the HDLC features, it seems appropriate to include information on HDLC. This appendix is organized into two parts. The first part explains the ISO data link service definitions. The second part explains the HDLC options.

SERVICE DEFINITIONS FOR THE LINK LAYER

In the main body of the text, I made reference to the use of service definitions and primitives, and how a programmer uses these tools to create software function calls. You may wish to refer back to Chapter 3, Figure 3–2 for this explanation.

The International Standards Organization (ISO) publishes a data link service definition in the DIS 8886 publication. The services are defined by primitives and DIS 8886 provides for both connection-oriented and connectionless services. These primitives are summarized in Tables A–1 and A–2.

Most of the primitives have associated parameters. These parameters are listed between parentheses with each of the primitive statements. The parameters are largely self-explanatory, for example, called address and calling address are used to identify the originator and receiver of the link layer traffic. Certain link-layer protocols support expe-

Table A–1   Connection-Oriented Service Definitions

DL-CONNECT.request	(Called Address, Calling Address, Expedited Data Selection, Quality of Service Parameters)
DL-CONNECT.indication	(Called Address, Calling Address, Expedited Data Selection, Quality of Service Parameters)
DL-CONNECT.response	(Responding Address, Expedited Data Selection, Quality of Service Parameters)
DL-CONNECT.confirm	(Responding Address, Expedited Data Selection, Quality of Service Parameters)
DL-DISCONNECT.request	(Originator, Reason)
DL-DISCONNECT.indication	(Originator, Reason)
DL-DATA.request	(User-Data
DL-DATA.indication	(User-Data)
DL-EXPEDITED-DATA.request	(User-Data)
DL-EXPEDITED-DATA.indication	(User-Data)
DL-RESET.request	(Originator, Reason)
DL-RESET.indication	(Originator, Reason)
DL-RESET.response	
DL-RESET.confirm	
DL-ERROR-REPORT.indication	(Reason)

dited data transfer. If this is the case, the parameter labeled expedited data selection can be used to invoke priority operations at the link layer.

The quality of service parameters allow a network layer to request certain types of services of the data-link layer. In actual implementations, the quality of services (QOS) parameters field is either left blank or contains relatively few values. This lack of QOS is because the data-link layer is a relatively low-function protocol and is not intended to provide very many sophisticated services.

Disconnects can be used by data-link layers to terminate the data-link connections. The originator provides its address in the disconnect and any reason for the disconnect in the reason field. The user data para-

Table A–2   Connectionless Service Definitions

DL-UNITDATA.request	(Source Address, Destination Address, Quality of Services, User Data)
DL-UNITDATA.indication	(Source Address, Destination Address, Quality of Services, User-Data)

meter is used to signify that end-user data from the network layer (and upper layers) are carried in the primitive.

The reader should keep in mind that these primitives and the parameters in the primitives are used to create the data-link control headers that are appended to the beginning and ending of user data—which results in the creation of the data link frame.

THE HDLC SCHEMA

Many other link protocols are derived from HDLC. Refer back to Chapter 2, Figure 2–1. While they are referred to as implementation options or subsets, they sometimes include other capabilities not found in HDLC. The major subsets are summarized in this section. The overall HDLC schema is shown in Figure A–1. The chart is read as follows.

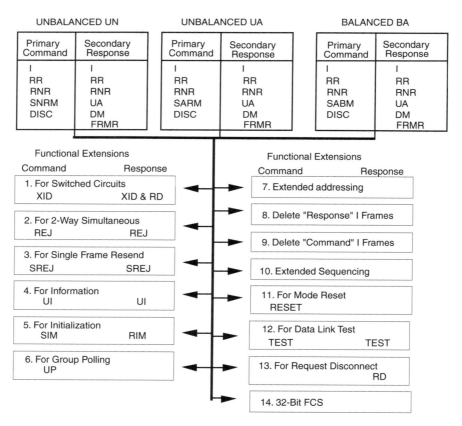

Figure A–1   HDLC Schema

The three boxes at the top of the figure show the three basic options for link configuration. Two options are provided for unbalanced links [Normal Response Mode (UN) and Asynchronous Response Mode (UA)] and one for balanced [Asynchronous Balanced Mode (BA)]. The boxes numbered 1–14 describe the functional extensions to the standard. These extensions allow the feature to be added as only a command frame or a response frame or either a command or a response frame. Several of the functional extensions do not relate to commands or responses. For example, functional extension 14 stipulates that a 32-bit frame check sequence field (FCS) is to be employed for error checking instead of the HDLC default of 16 bits.

Table A–3   HDLC Control Field Format (Modulo 8)

Format	*Control Field Bit Encoding*								Commands	Responses
	1	**2**	**3**	**4**	**5**	**6**	**7**	**8**		
Information	0	–	N(S)	–		–	N(R)	–	I	I
Supervisory	1	0	0	0	•	–	N(R)	–	RR	RR
	1	0	0	1	•	–	N(R)	–	REJ	REJ
	1	0	1	0	•	–	N(R)	–	RNR	RNR
	1	0	1	1	•	–	N(R)	–	SREJ	SREJ
Unnumbered	1	1	0	0	•	0	0	0	UI	UI
	1	1	0	0	•	0	0	1	SNRM	
	1	1	0	0	•	0	1	0	DISC	RD
	1	1	0	0	•	1	0	0	UP	
	1	1	0	0	•	1	1	0		UA
	1	1	0	1	•	0	0	0	NR0	NR0
	1	1	0	1	•	0	0	1	NR1	NR1
	1	1	0	1	•	0	1	0	NR2	NR2
	1	1	0	1	•	0	1	1	NR3	NR3
	1	1	1	0	•	0	0	0	SIM	RIM
	1	1	1	0	•	0	0	1		FRMR
	1	1	1	1	•	0	0	0	SARM	DM
	1	1	1	1	•	0	0	1	RSET	
	1	1	1	1	•	0	1	0	SARME	
	1	1	1	1	•	0	1	1	SNRME	
	1	1	1	1	•	1	0	0	SABM	
	1	1	1	1	•	1	0	1	XID	XID
	1	1	1	1	•	1	1	0	SABME	

Table A–3 *Continued*

Legend:

I	Information	NR0	Non-Reserved 0
RR	Receive Ready	NR1	Non-Reserved 1
REJ	Reject	NR2	Non-Reserved 2
RNR	Receive Not Ready	NR3	Non-Reserved 3
SREJ	Selective Reject	SIM	Set Initialization Mode
UI	Unnumbered Information	RIM	Request Initialization Mode
SNRM	Set Normal Response Mode	FRMR	Frame Reject
DISC	Disconnect	SARM	Set Async Response Mode
RD	Request Disconnect	SARME	Set ARM Extended Mode
UP	Unnumbered Poll	SNRM	Set Normal Response Mode
RSET	Reset	SNRME	Set NRM Extended Mode
XID	Exchange Identification	SABM	Set Async Balance Mode
DM	Disconnect Mode	SABME	Set ABM Extended Mode
•	The P/F Bit		

In order to classify a protocol conveniently, the terms UN, UA, and BA are used to denote which subset of HDLC is used. In addition, most subsets use the functional extensions. For example, a protocol classified as UN 3,7 uses the unbalanced normal response mode option and the selective reject and extended address functional extensions.

Table A–3 shows the HDLC commands and responses. The bits of the control field for modulo 8 sequencing are also depicted, as are information, supervisory, and unnumbered frames.

Table A–4 provides more detail on the control field of the HDLC frames.

Table A–4   HDLC Frame Types

- *Receive Ready (RR):* Indicates station is ready to receive traffic and/or acknowledge previously received frames by using the N(R) field.
- *Receive Not Ready (RNR):* Indicates to the transmitting station that the receiving station is unwilling to accept additional incoming data. The RNR frame may acknowledge previously transmitted frames by using the N(R) field.
- *Selective Reject (SREJ):* Requests the retransmission of a single frame identified in the N(R) field. All information frames numbered up to N(R)-1 are acknowledged.
- *Reject (REJ):* Requests the retransmission of frames starting with the frame numbered in the N(R) field.
- *Unnumbered Information (UI):* Allows for transmission of user data in an unnumbered (i.e., unsequenced) frame.
- *Request Initialization Mode (RIM):* Requests from a secondary station for initialization to a primary station.
- *Set Normal Response Mode (SNRM):* Places the secondary station in the Normal Response Mode (NRM).
- *Disconnect (DISC):* Places the station in the disconnected mode.
- *Disconnect Mode (DM):* Transmitted to indicate a station is in the disconnect mode (not operational).
- *Test (TEST):* Used to solicit testing responses from a station.
- *Set Asynchronous Response Mode (SARM):* Allows a secondary station to transmit without a poll from the primary station.
- *Set Asynchronous Balanced Mode (SABM):* Sets mode to ABM, in which stations are peers with each other.
- *Set Normal Response Mode Extended (SNRME):* Sets SNRM with two octets in the control field. This is used for extended sequencing and permits the N(S) and N(R) to be seven bits in length, thus increasing the window to a range of 1–127.
- *Set Asynchronous Balanced Mode Extended (SABME):* Sets SABM with two octets in the control field for extended sequencing.
- *Unnumbered Poll (UP):* Polls a station without regard to sequencing or acknowledgment.
- *Reset (RESET):* Used for reinitialization. Previously unacknowledged frames remain unacknowledged.
- *Request Disconnect (RD):* Used to request a disconnection

Appendix B
The Internet: Architecture

INTRODUCTION

This appendix is an introduction to the Internet's architecture and its layered protocol suites. The material is written for the person who is new to TCP/IP and Internet protocols.

THE PROTOCOL SUITE

Figure B–1 depicts an architectural model of TCP/IP and several of the major related protocols. The choices in the stacking of the layers of this model vary, depending on the needs of network users and the decisions made by network designers. IP is the key protocol at the network layer. Several other protocols are used in conjunction with IP that serve as route discovery and address mapping protocols. The protocols that rest over TCP (and UDP) are examples of the application layer protocols.

The lower two layers represent the data link and physical layers, are implemented with a wide choice of standards and protocols. This book has concentrated on PPP, which operates at the data-link layer.

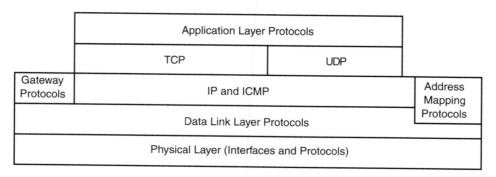

Figure B–1   The TCP/IP (Internet Model)

The Physical Layer

The lowest layer in the Internet model is called the physical layer (layer 1 or L_1), although these standards do not dictate the interfaces and protocols that reside in this layer. The functions within the layer are identical to the OSI Model and are responsible for activating, maintaining, and deactivating a physical circuit between machines. This layer defines the type of physical signals (electrical, optical, etc.), as well as the type of media (wires, coaxial cable, satellite, etc.).

There are many standards published for the physical layer; for example EIA-232-E, V.34, V.35, and V.90 are physical layer protocols. The TCP/IP suite is implemented widely on local area networks (LANs), usually above the IEEE 802 or ISO 8802 standards.

The Data-Link Layer

The data-link layer (layer 2 or L_2) is responsible for the transfer of data across one communications link. It delimits the flow of bits from the physical layer. It also provides for the identity of the bits. It usually ensures that the data arrives safely at the receiving DTE. It often provides for flow control to ensure that the DTE does not become overburdened with too much data at any one time. One of its most important functions is to provide for the detection of transmission errors and provide mechanisms to recover from lost, duplicated, or erroneous data.

Common examples of data link control (DLC) protocols are the High-Level Data Link Control (HDLC), published by the ISO; Synchronous Data Link Control (SDLC), used by IBM; and the Point-to-Point Protocol (PPP).

The Network Layer

The Internet Protocol (IP) is a simple protocol operating at the network layer, layer 3, or L_3. It routes traffic between networks. IP is quite similar to the ISO 8473 (the Connectionless Network Protocol or CLNP) specification, which is the OSI counterpart to IP. Many of the ISO 8473 concepts were derived from IP.

IP is an example of a connectionless service. It permits the exchange of traffic between two host computers without any prior call setup. It is possible that data could be lost between the two end-user's stations. For example, the IP gateway enforces a maximum queue length size, and if this queue length is violated, the buffers will overflow. In this situation, the additional datagrams are discarded in the network.

The IP has no error-reporting or error-correcting mechanisms. It relies on a module called the Internet Control Message Protocol (ICMP) to (a) report errors in the processing of a datagram, and (b) provide for some administrative and status messages.

The ICMP will notify the host if a destination is unreachable. ICMP is also responsible for managing or creating a time-exceeded message in the event that the lifetime of the datagram expires. ICMP also performs certain editing functions to determine if the IP header is in error or otherwise unintelligible.

IP is not a route discovery protocol, but a forwarding protocol. It makes use of the routing tables that are filled in by gateway protocols; one of which (OSPF) operates directly with the IP header (that is, it does not run on TCP or UDP). The purpose of these protocols is to "find" a good route for the traffic to traverse through an internet. The vast majority of gateway protocols route traffic based on the idea that it makes the best sense to transmit the datagram through the fewest number of networks and gateways (hops). The newer protocols use other criteria such as finding the route with the best throughput or the shortest delay. These newer gateway protocols use adaptive and dynamic methods to update the routing tables to reflect traffic and link conditions.

Layer_2 and Layer_3 Address Resolution Operations

The IP stack provides a protocol for resolving addresses. The Address Resolution Protocol (ARP) is used to take care of the translation of IP addresses to physical addresses and hide these physical addresses from the upper layers.

Generally, ARP works with mapping tables (referred to as the ARP cache). The table provides the mapping between an IP address and a physical address. In a LAN (like Ethernet or an IEEE 802 network), ARP takes an IP address and searches for a corresponding physical address in a mapping table. If it finds the address, it returns the physical address back to the requester, such as a server on a LAN. However, if the needed address is not found in the ARP cache, the ARP module sends a broadcast onto the network.

Another protocol, called Proxy ARP, allows an organization to use only one IP address (network portion of address) for multiple networks. In essence, Proxy ARP maps a single IP network address into multiple physical addresses.

The ARP protocol is a useful technique for determining physical addresses from network addresses. However, some workstations do not know their own IP address. For example, diskless workstations do not have any IP address knowledge when they are booted to a system. The diskless workstations know only their hardware address. The Reverse Address Resolution Protocol (RARP) works in a manner similar to ARP except, as the name suggests, it works in reverse order: It provides an IP address when given a MAC address. RARP is often used on LANs for booting the machines to the network.

The Transport Layer

The Transmission Control Protocol (TCP) resides in the transport layer (layer 4 or L_4) of the Internet Model. It is situated above IP and below the upper layers. It is designed to reside in the host computer or in a machine that is tasked with end-to-end integrity of the transfer of user data.

Since IP is a connectionless network, the tasks of reliability, flow control, sequencing, opens, and closes are given to TCP. Although TCP and IP are tied together so closely that they are used in the same context "TCP/IP," TCP can also support other protocols.

The User Datagram Protocol (UDP) is classified as a connectionless protocol. It is sometimes used in place of TCP in situations where the full services of TCP are not needed. For example the Trivial File Transfer Protocol (TFTP), and the Remote Procedure Call (RPC) use UDP.

UDP serves as a simple application interface to the IP. Since it has no reliability, flow control, nor error-recovery measures, it serves principally as a multiplexer/demultiplexer for the receiving and sending of IP traffic.

The Application Layer

The Internet application layer (layer 7 or L_7) protocols serve as a direct service provider to user applications and workstations. Operations, such as electronic mail, file transfer, name servers, and terminal services are provided in this layer.

Some of the more widely-used application layer services include:

- *Trivial File Transfer Protocol (TFTP):* For simple file transfer services
- *File Transfer Protocol (FTP):* For more elaborate file transfer services
- *Simple Mail Transfer Protocol (SMTP):* For message transfer services (electronic mail)
- *Domain Name System (DNS):* For name server operations
- *Browsers*
- *Simple Network Management Protocol (SNMP):* For network management operations

NAMES AND ADDRESSES

A newcomer to data networks is often perplexed when the subject of naming and addressing arises. Addresses in data networks are similar to postal addresses and telephone numbering schemes. Indeed, many of the networks that exist today have derived some of their addressing structures from the concepts of the telephone numbering plan.

It should prove useful to clarify the meaning of names, addresses, and routes. A *name* is an identification of an entity (independent of its physical location), such as a person, an applications program, or even a computer. An *address* is also an identification but it reveals additional information about the entity, principally information about its physical or logical placement in a network. A *route* is information on how to relay traffic to a physical location (address).

A network usually provides a service which allows a network user to furnish the network with a name of something (another user, an application, etc.) that is to receive traffic. A network *name server* then uses this name to determine the address of the receiving entity. This address is then used by a routing protocol to determine the physical route to the receiver.

With this approach, a network user does not become involved and is not aware of physical addresses and the physical location of other users and network resources. This practice allows the network administrator to relocate, and reconfigure network resources without affecting end users. Likewise, users can move to other physical locations but their names remain the same. The network changes its naming/routing tables to reflect the relocation.

Chapter 1 emphasized that the evolution of WANs and LANs occurred separately. Consequently, two different addresses were developed; one to identify WAN entities and another to identify LAN entities. Because these addresses play an important role in this book, they are examined in the next section.

Physical Addresses

Communications between users through a data network requires several forms of addressing. Typically, two addresses are required: (a) a physical address, also called a data link address, and (b) a network address. Other identifiers are needed for unambiguous end-to-end communications between two users, such as upper layer names and/or port addresses.

Each device (such as a computer or workstation) on a communications link or network is identified with a physical address. This address is also called the hardware address. Many manufacturers place the physical address on a logic board within the device or in an interface unit connected directly to the device. Two physical addresses are employed in a communications dialogue, one address identifies the sender (source) and the other address identifies the receiver (destination). The length of the physical address varies, and most implementations use two 48-bit addresses.

The address detection operation on a LAN is illustrated in Figure B–2. Device A transmits a frame onto the channel. It is received by all other stations attached to the channel, namely stations B, C, and D. We assume that the destination physical address contains the value C. Consequently, stations B and D ignore the frame. Station C accepts it, performs several tasks associated with the physical layer, strips away the physical layer headers and trailers, and passes the remainder of the packet to the next upper layer.

The MAC Address. The IEEE assigns LAN addresses. Previously this work was performed by the Xerox Corporation by administering

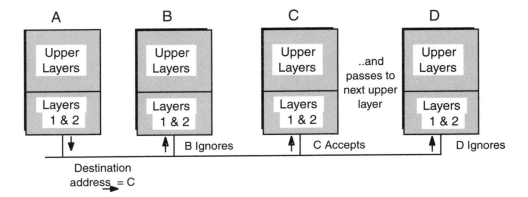

Figure B–2   Physical address detection

Notes:
For LANs, address is called a MAC address
For non-LAN links, address is called a link address, or some
variation of an "HDLC" address
Where:
    HDLC   High level data link control
    MAC   Media access control

what were known as block identifiers (Block IDs) for Ethernet addresses. The Xerox Ethernet Administration Office assigned these values, which were three octets (24 bits) in length. The organization that received this address was free to use the remaining 24 bits of the Ethernet address in any way it chose.

Due to the progress made in the IEEE 802 project, it was decided that the IEEE would assume the task of assigning these universal identifiers for all LANs, not just CSMA/CD types of networks. However, the IEEE continues to honor the assignments made by the Ethernet administration office although it now calls the block ID an *organization unique identifier (OUI)*.

The format for the OUI is shown in Figure B–3. The least significant bit of the address space corresponds to the individual/group (I/G) address bit. The I/G address bit, if set to a zero, means that the address field identifies an individual address. If the value is set to a one, the address field identifies a group address which is used to identify more than one station connected to the LAN. If the entire OUI is set to all ones, it signifies a broadcast address which identifies all stations on the network.

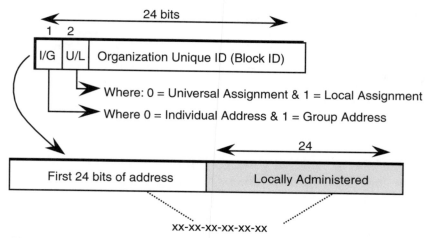

Note: Format of xx represents an octet, with each x 4 bits:
A2-59-ED-18-F5-7C

Figure B–3   Universal addresses and IDs: The MAC address

The second bit of the address space is the local or universal bit (U/L). When this bit is set to a zero, it has universal assignment significance—for example, from the IEEE. If it is set to a one it is an address that is locally assigned. Bit position number two must always be set to a zero if it is administered by the IEEE.

The OUI is extended to include a 48 bit universal LAN address (which is designated as the *media access control [MAC]* address). The 24 bits of the address space is the same as the OUI assigned by the IEEE. The one exception is that the I/G bit may be set to a one or a zero to identify group or individual addresses. The second part of the address space consisting of the remaining 24 bits is locally administered and can be set to any values an organization chooses.

The Network Address

A network address (or network layer address) identifies a network, or networks. Part of the network address may also designate a computer, a terminal, or anything that a private network administrator wishes to identify within a network (or attached to a network), although the Internet standards place very strict rules on what an IP address identifies.

A network address is a "higher level" address than the physical address. The components in an internet that deal with network addresses need not be concerned with physical addresses until the data has arrived at the network link to which the physical device is attached.

This important concept is illustrated in Figure B–4. Assume that a user (host computer) in Los Angeles transmits packets to a packet network for relaying to a workstation on a LAN in London. The network in London has a network address of XYZ (this address scheme is explained shortly).

The packets are passed through the packet network (using the network's internal routing mechanisms) to the packet switch in New York. The packet switch in New York routes the packet to the gateway located in London. This gateway examines the destination network address in the packet and determines that the packet is to be routed to network XYZ. It then transmits the packet onto the appropriate communications channel (link) to the node on the LAN that is responsible for communicating with the London gateway.

Notice that this operation did not use any physical addresses in these routing operations. The packet switches and gateway were only concerned with the destination network address of XYZ.

The reader might question how the London LAN is able to pass the packet to the correct device (host). As we learned earlier, a physical address is needed to prevent every packet from being processed by the

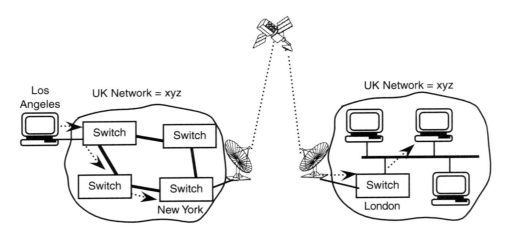

Figure B–4   Network layer addressing

upper-layer network-layer protocols residing in every host attached to the network. Therefore, the answer is that the target network (or gateway) must be able to translate a higher layer network destination address to a lower layer physical destination address.

In Figure B–5, a node on the LAN is a server that is tasked with address resolution. Let us assume that the destination address contains a network address, such as 128.1 *and* a host address, say 3.2. Therefore, the two addresses could be joined (concatenated) to create a full internet network address, which would appear as 128.1.3.2 in the destination address field of the IP datagram.

Once the LAN node receives the datagram from the gateway, it must examine the host address, and either (a) perform a look-up into a table that contains the local physical address and its associated network address, or (b) query the station for its physical address. Then, it encapsulates the user data into the LAN frame, places the appropriate LAN physical layer address in the destination address of the frame, and transmits the frame onto the LAN channel. All devices on the network examine the physical address. If this address matches the device's address, the PDU is passed to the next upper layer; otherwise, it is ignored.

In this manner the two addresses can be associated with each other.

The IP Address.   TCP/IP networks use a 32-bit network layer-3 address to identify a host computer and the network to which the host is at-

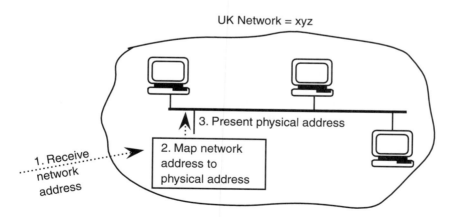

Figure B–5   Mapping network addresses to physical addresses

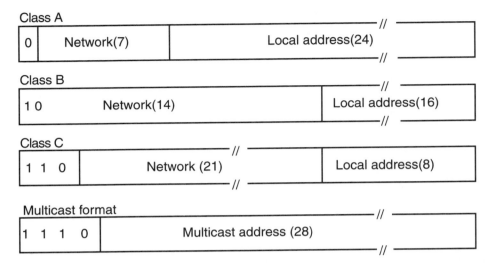

Figure B–6 shown: Class A, Class B, Class C, and Multicast format.

Class A

| 0 | Network(7) | Local address(24) | // |

Class B

| 1 0 | Network(14) | Local address(16) | // |

Class C

| 1 1 0 | Network (21) | Local address(8) | // |

Multicast format

| 1 1 1 0 | Multicast address (28) | // |

Note: Internet Network Information Center (InterNIC) assigns addresses: Contact: rs.internic.net

Figure B–6   Internet Protocol (IP) address formats

tached. The structure of the IP address is depicted in Figure B–6. Its format is:

$$\text{IP address} = \text{network address} + \text{host address}$$

The IP address identifies a host's connection to its network; that is, a point of attachment. Consequently, if a host machine is moved to another network, its address must be changed. This aspect of the IP address has major implications for mobile systems, discussed in Chapter 11.

In the past, IP addresses have been classified by their formats:[1] class-A, class-B, class-C, or class-D formats. As illustrated in Figure B–6, the first bits of the address specify the format of the remainder of the address field in relation to the network and host subfields. The host address is also called the local address (also called the REST field).

The *class-A* addresses provide for networks that have a large number of hosts. The host ID field is 24 bits. Therefore, 2^{24} hosts can be identified. Seven bits are devoted to the network ID, which supports an identification scheme for as many as 127 networks (bit values of 1 to 127).

---

[1]I say, in the past, but this system still prevails. Yet, it is being replaced by a concept called classless addresses, a topic explained in Chapter 7.

Class-B addresses are used for networks of intermediate size. Fourteen bits are assigned for the network ID, and 16 bits are assigned for the host ID. *Class-C* networks contain fewer than 256 hosts (2^8). Twenty-one bits are assigned to the network ID. Finally, *class-D* addresses are reserved for multicasting, which is a form of broadcasting but within a limited area.

The IP address space can take the following forms as shown in Figure B–7, and the maximum network and host addresses that are available for the class A, B, and C addresses are also shown.

There are instances when an organization has no need to connect into the Internet or another private intranet. Therefore, it is not necessary to adhere to the IP addressing registration conventions, and the organization can use the addresses it chooses. It is important that it is certain that connections to other networks will not occur, since the use of addresses that are allocated elsewhere could create problems.

In RFC 1597, several IP addresses have been allocated for private addresses, and it is a good idea to use these addresses if an organization chooses not to register with the Internet. Systems are available that will

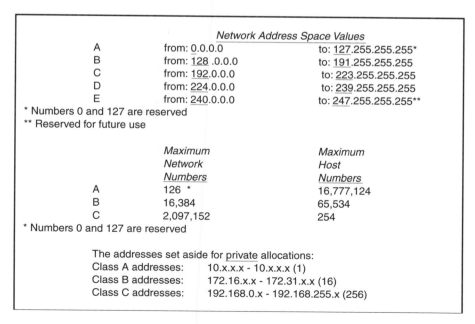

Figure B–7   IP addresses

translate private, unregistered addresses to public, registered addresses if connections to global systems are needed.

Figure B–8 shows examples of the assignment of IP address in more detail (examples use IP class-B addresses). A common backbone (Common Net) connects three subnetworks: 176.16.2, 176.16.3, and 176.16.4. Routers act as the interworking units between the legacy (conventional) LANs and the backbone. The backbone could be a conventional Ethernet, but in most situations, the backbone is a Fiber Distributed Data Interface (FDDI), a Fast Ethernet node, or an ATM hub.

The routers are also configured as subnet nodes and access servers are installed in the network to support address and naming information services.

ARP

Earlier discussions in this Appendix covered the need to correlate a host's MAC and IP addresses and the IP protocol stack provides a protocol to support this operation. The Address Resolution Protocol (ARP) is

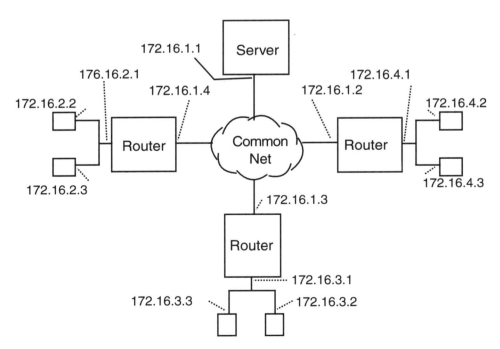

Figure B–8   Examples of IP addressing

used to take care of the translation of IP addresses to physical addresses and hide these physical addresses from the upper layers.

Generally, ARP works with mapping tables (referred to as the ARP cache). The table provides the mapping between an IP address and a physical address. In a LAN (like Ethernet or an IEEE 802 network), ARP takes the target IP address and searches for a corresponding physical address in a mapping table. If it finds the address, it returns the 48-bit address back to the requester, such as a device driver or server on a LAN. However, if the needed address is not found in the ARP cache, the ARP module sends a broadcast onto the network.

The broadcast is called the *ARP request*. The ARP request contains an IP address. Consequently, if one of the machines receiving the broadcast recognizes its IP address in the ARP request, it will return an ARP reply back to the inquiring host. This datagram contains the physical hardware address of the queried host. Upon receiving this datagram, the inquiring host places this address into the ARP cache. Thereafter, data-

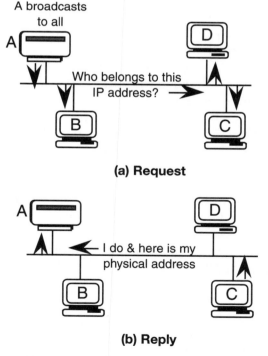

(a) Request

(b) Reply

Figure B–9   The ARP request and reply

grams sent to this particular IP address can be translated to the physical address.

The ARP system thus allows an inquiring host to find the physical address of another host by using the IP address.

The concepts of ARP requests and replies are shown in Figure B–9. Host A wishes to determine C's physical address. It broadcasts datagrams (all 1s in the MAC destination address) to B, C, and D. Only C responds because it recognizes its IP address in the incoming ARP request datagram. Host C places its address into an IP datagram in the form of the ARP reply. The other hosts, B and D, do not respond.

A BRIEF LOOK AT IP

I mentioned that it is not the intent of this book to describe in detail the current Internet Protocols. So, a productive approach to a general analysis of IP is to examine the fields in the IP datagram (PDU) depicted in Figure B–10.

The *version* field identifies the version of IP in use. Most protocols contain this field because some network nodes may not have the latest release available of the protocol. The current version of IP is 4, or IPv4.

The *header length* field contains 4 bits which are set to a value to indicate the length of the datagram header. The length is measured in 32-bit words. Typically, a header without QOS options contains 20 octets. Therefore, the value in the length field is usually 5.

The *total length* field specifies the total length of the IP datagram. It is measured in octets and includes the length of the header and the data. IP subtracts the header length field from the total length field to compute the size of the data field. The maximum possible length of a datagram is 65,535 octets (2^{16}). Gateways that service IP datagrams are required to accept any datagram that supports the maximum size of a PDU of the attached networks. Additionally, all gateways must accommodate datagrams of 576 octets in total length.

Each 32-bit value is transmitted in this order: (a) bits 0–7, (b) bits 8–15, (c) bits 16–23, and (d) bits 24–31. This is known as big endian byte ordering.

Type of Service (TOS)

The *type of service* (TOS) field can be used to identify several QOS functions provided for an Internet application. It is quite similar to the

									1	1			2	2		3
0	1-2	3	4	5-6	7	8	9-15		5	6	17-22		3	4	25-30	1
Version		H-Length		Type of Service (TOS)						Total Length						
Identifier									Flags			Fragment Offset				
Time to Live				Protocol					Header Checksum							
Source Address (32)																
Destination Address (32)																
Options and Padding (Variable)																
Data (Variable)																

Where:
  H-Length   Header Length

Figure B–10   The IP datagram

service field that resides in the OSI-based CLNP (Connectionless Network Protocol) PDU. Transit delay, throughput, precedence, and reliability can be requested with this field.

The TOS field contains five entries consisting of 8 bits. Bits 0, 1, and 2 contain a precedence value which is used to indicate the relative importance of the datagram. Values range from 0 to 7, with 0 set to indicate a *routine precedence*. The precedence field is not used in most systems, although the value of 7 is used by some implementations to indicate a network control datagram. However, the precedence field could be used to implement flow control and congestion mechanisms in a network. This would allow gateways and host nodes to make decisions about the order of "throwing away" datagrams in case of congestion.

The next three bits are used for other services and are described as follows: Bit 3 is the *delay bit* (D bit). When set to 1 this TOS requests a short delay through an internet. The aspect of delay is not defined in the standard and it is up to the vendor to implement the service. The next bit is the *throughput bit* (T bit). It is set to 1 to request for high throughput through an internet. Again, its specific implementation is not defined in the standard. The next bit used is the *reliability bit* (R bit), which allows a user to request high reliability for the datagram. The last bit of interest is the *cost bit* (C bit), which is set to request the use of a low-cost link (from the standpoint of monetary cost). The last bit is not used at this time.

The *TOS field* is not used in some vendors' implementation of IP. Nonetheless, it will be used increasingly in the future as the internet capabilities are increased. For example, it is used in the Open Shortest Path First (OSPF) protocol. Consequently, a user should examine this field for future work and ascertain a vendor's use or intended support of this field.

Fragmentation Fields

The IP protocol uses three fields in the header to control datagram fragmentation and reassembly. These fields are the *identifier*, *flags*, and *fragmentation offset*. The identifier field is used to uniquely identify all fragments from an original datagram. It is used with the source address at the receiving host to identify the fragment. The flags field contains bits to determine if the datagram may be fragmented, and if fragmented, one of the bits can be set to determine if this fragment is the last fragment of the datagram. The fragmentation offset field contains a value which specifies the relative position of the fragment to the original datagram. The value is initialized as 0 and is subsequently set to the proper number if/when an IP node fragments the data. The value is measured in units of eight octets.

Time-to-live (TTL) Field

The *time-to-live* (TTL) field is used to measure the time a datagram has been in the internet. Each gateway in the internet is required to check this field and discard the datagram if the TTL value equals 0. An IP node is also required to decrement this field in each datagram it processes. In actual implementations, the TTL field is a number of hops value. Therefore, when a datagram proceeds through a gateway (hop), the value in the field is decremented by a value of one. Some implementations of IP use a time-counter in this field and decrement the value in one-second decrements.

The TTL field is used not only to prevent endless loops, it can also be used by the host to limit the lifetime that datagrams have in an internet. Be aware that if a host is acting as a "route-through" node, it must treat the TTL field by the router rules. The seminar attendee should check with the vendor to determine when a host throws away a datagram based on the TTL value.

Ideally, the TTL value could be configured and its value assigned based on observing an internet's performance. Additionally, network management information protocols such as those residing in SNMP might wish to set the TTL value for diagnostic purposes. Finally, if your vendor uses a fixed value that cannot be reconfigured, make certain that it is fixed initially to allow for your internet's growth.

Protocol Field

The *protocol* field is used to identify the next protocol that is to receive the datagram at the final host destination. It is similar to the Ethertype field found in the Ethernet frame, but identifies the payload in the data field of the IP datagram. The Internet standards groups have established a numbering system to identify the most widely used protocols that "reside" in the IP datagram data field.

Header Checksum

The *header checksum* is used to detect an error that may have occurred in the header. Checks are not performed on the user data stream. Some critics of IP have stated that the provision for error detection in the user data should allow the receiving gateway to at least notify the sending host that problems have occurred. (This service is indeed provided by a companion standard to IP [the ICMP.]) Whatever one's view on the issue, the current approach keeps the checksum algorithm in IP quite simple. It does not have to operate on many octets, but it does require that a higher level protocol at the receiving host must perform some type of error check on the user data if it cares about its integrity.

The checksum is computed as follows (and this same procedure is used in TCP, UDP, ICMP, and IGMP):

- Set checksum field to 0.
- Calculate 16-bit one's complement sum of the header (header is treated as a sequence of 16-bit words).
- Store 16-bit one's complement in the checksum field.
- At receiver, calculate 16-bit one's complement of the header.
- Receiver's checksum is all 1s if the header has not been changed.

Address Fields

IP carries two addresses in the datagram. These are labeled *source* and *destination addresses* and remain the same value throughout the life of the datagram. These fields contain the Internet addresses, described earlier in this chapter.

Options Field

The *options* field is used to identify several additional services[2] (see Figure B–11). The options field is not used in every datagram. The majority of implementations use this field for network management and diagnostics. Many implementations do not even use this field.

The options field length is variable because some options are of variable length. Each option contains three fields. The first field is coded as a single octet containing the option code. The option code also contains three fields. Their functions are as follows:

- *Flag copy (1 bit):*   0 = Copy option into only the first fragment of a fragmented datagram
  1 = Copy option into all fragments of a fragmented datagram
- *Class (2 bits):*   Identifies the option class
- *Option Number:*   Identifies the option number

The option class can be set to the following values:

- *0:* A user datagram or a network control datagram
- *1:* Reserved
- *2:* Diagnostics purposes (debugging and measuring)
- *3:* Reserved

The next octet contains the length of the option. The third field contains the data values for the option. The *padding* field may be used to make certain that the datagram header aligns on an exact 32-bit boundary.

IP provides two options in routing the datagram to the final destination. The first, called *loose source routing*, gives the IP nodes the option of

---

[2]The option field has fallen into disuse by routers, because of the processing overhead required to support the features it identifies. The concepts of this field are well-founded, and a similar capability is found in IPv6, discussed in Chapter 8.

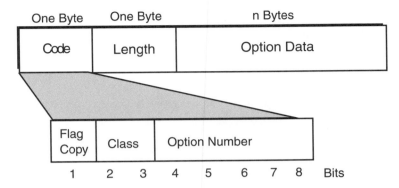

Figure B–11   The IP option field and option codes

using intermediate hops to reach the addresses obtained in the source list as long as the datagram traverses the nodes listed. Conversely, *strict source routing* requires that the datagram travel only through the networks whose addresses are indicated in the source list. If the strict source route cannot be followed, the originating host IP is notified with an error message. Both loose and strict routing require that the route recording feature be implemented.

An Overview of Fragmentation

An IP datagram may traverse a number of different networks that use different frame sizes, and all networks have a maximum frame size, called the maximum transmission unit (MTU). Therefore, IP contains procedures for dividing (fragmenting) a large datagram into smaller datagrams. It also allows the ULP to stipulate that fragmentation may or may not occur. Of course, it must also use a reassembly mechanism at the final destination which places the fragments back into the order originally transmitted.

When an IP gateway module receives a datagram which is too big to be transmitted by the transit subnetwork, it uses its fragmentation operations. It divides the datagram into two or more pieces. Each of the fragmented pieces has a header attached containing identification, addressing, and as another option, all options pertaining to the original datagram. The fragmented packets also have information attached to them defining the position of the fragment within the original datagram, as well as an indication if this fragment is the last fragment. The flags (the 3 bits) are used as follows:

- *Bit 0* = reserved
- *Bit 1; 0* = fragmentation and 1 = don't fragment
- *Bit 2 (M bit)*; 0 = last fragment and 1 = more fragments

Interestingly, IP handles each fragment operation independently. That is to say, the fragments may traverse different paths to the intended destination, and they may be subject to further fragmentation if they pass through networks that use smaller data units. The next node uses the offset value in the incoming fragment to determine the offset values of fragmented datagrams. If further fragmentation is done at another node, the fragment offset value is set to the location that this fragment fits relative to the original datagram and not the preceding fragmented packet.

A BRIEF LOOK AT TCP AND UDP

The Transmission Control Protocol (TCP) and the user datagram protocol (UDP) operate at layer 4 of the Internet protocol stack. TCP is a connection-oriented protocol, and is responsible for the reliable transfer of user traffic between two hosts. Consequently, it uses sequence numbers and acknowledgments to make certain all traffic is delivered safely to the destination end-point.

UDP is a connectionless protocol and does not provide sequencing or acknowledgments. It is used in place of TCP in situations where the full services of TCP are not needed. For example, telephony traffic, the Trivial File Transfer Protocol (TFTP), and the Remote Procedure Call (RPC) use UDP. Since it has no reliability, flow control, nor error-recovery measures, UDP serves principally as a multiplexer/demultiplexer for the receiving and sending of traffic into and out of an application.

The packets exchanged between two TCP modules are called segments. Figure B–12 illustrates the format for the segment.

The first two fields of the segment are identified as *source port* and *destination port*. These 16-bit fields are used to identify the upper layer application programs that are using the TCP connection.

The next field is labeled *sequence number*. This field contains the sequence number of the first octet in the user data field. Its value specifies the position of the transmitting module's byte stream. Within the segment, it specifies the first user data octet in the segment.

The sequence number is also used during a connection management operation. If a connection request segment is used between two TCP entities, the sequence number specifies the *initial send sequence* (ISS) number that is to be used for the subsequent numbering of the user data.

The *acknowledgment number* is set to a value which acknowledges data previously received. The value in this field contains the value of the sequence number of the next expected octet from the transmitter. Since this number is set to the next expected octet, it provides an inclusive acknowledgment capability, in that it acknowledges all octets up to and including this number, minus 1.

The *data offset* field specifies the number of 32-bit aligned words that comprise the TCP header. This field is used to determine where the data field begins.

As the reader might expect, the *reserved* field is reserved. It consists of 6-bits which must be set to zero. These bits are reserved for future use.

The next six fields are called flags. They are labeled as control bits by TCP and they are used to specify certain services and operations which are to be used during the session. Some of the bits determine how to interpret other fields in the header. The six bits are used to convey the following information:

- *URG (U):* This flag signifies if the urgent pointer field is significant.
- *ACK (A):* This flag signifies if the acknowledgment field is significant.

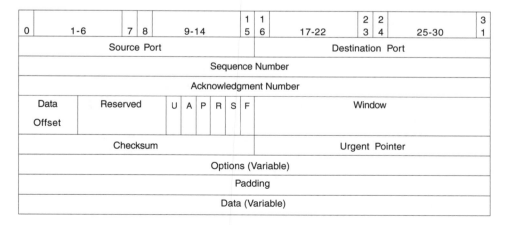

Figure B–12   The TCP segment (PDU)

- *PSH (P)*: This flag signifies that the module is to exercise the push function. Some systems do not support the push function, but rely on TCP to "push" the traffic efficiently.
- *RST (R)*: This flag indicates that the connection is to be reset.
- *SYN (S)*: This flag is used to indicate that the sequence numbers are to be synchronized; it is used with the connection-establishment segments as a flag to indicate handshaking operations are to take place.
- *FIN (F)*: This flag indicates that the sender has no more data to send and is comparable to the end-of-transmission (EOT) signal in other protocols.

The next field is labeled *window*. This value is set to a value indicating how many octets the receiver is willing to accept. The value is established based on the value in the acknowledgment field (acknowledgment number). The window is established by adding the value in the window field to the value of the acknowledgment number field.

The *checksum* field performs a 16-bit one's complement of the one's complement sum of all the 16-bit words in the segment. This includes the header and the text. The purpose of the checksum calculation is to determine if the segment has arrived error-free from the transmitter.

The next field in the segment is labeled the *urgent pointer*. This field is only used if the URG flag is set. The purpose of the urgent pointer is to signify the data octet in which urgent data follows. Urgent data is also called *out-of-band* data. TCP does not dictate what happens for urgent data. It is implementation specific. It only signifies where the urgent data is located. It is an offset from the sequence number and points to the octet following the urgent data.

The *options* field was conceived to provide for future enhancements to TCP. It is constructed in a manner similar to that of IP datagrams option field, in that each option specification consists of a single byte containing an option number, a field containing the length of the option, and last the option values themselves.

Presently the option field is limited in its use, but options are available dealing with size of the TCP data field, window size, a timestamp for an echo, and some others under consideration. For more information, see RFC 1323.

Finally, the *padding* field is used to insure that the TCP header is filled to an even multiple of 32 bits. After that, as the figure illustrates, user *data* follows.

The options field in the TCP header can contain a number of options, and the original specification included only the maximum segment size (MSS) option. This option is almost universal, and is found in practically all TCP SYN segments. The MSS value permits the two TCP entities to inform each other about the size of their traffic units, and to reserve buffer of their reception. The other options are relatively new, and their implementation will depend upon the TCP product. For more information, see RFCs 793, and 1323.

The TCP Open Operation

Figure B–13 illustrates the major operations between two TCP entities to establish a connection.

TCP A's user has sent an active open primitive to TCP. The remote user has sent a passive open to its TCP provider. These operations are listed as events 2 and 1 respectively, although either event could have occurred in either order.

The invocation of the active open requires TCP A to prepare a segment with the SYN bit set to 1. The segment is sent to TCP B and is depicted in the figure as 3 and coded as: SYN SEQ 100. In this example, sequence (SEQ) number 100 is used as the ISS number although any number could be chosen within the rules discussed earlier. The SYN coding simply means the SYN bit is set to the value of 1.

Upon receiving the SYN segment, TCP B returns an acknowledgment with sequence number of 101. It also sends its ISS number of 177. This event is labeled as 4.

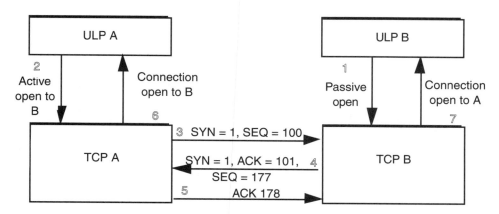

Figure B–13   TCP open operations

Upon the receipt of this segment, TCP A acknowledges with a segment containing the acknowledgment number of 178. This is depicted as event 5 in the figure.

Once these handshaking operations have occurred with events 3, 4, and 5 (which is called a three-way handshake), the two TCP modules send opens to their respective users as in events 6 and 7.

TCP Data Transfer Operations

Figure B–14 shows the TCP entities after they have successfully achieved a connection. In event 1, ULP A sends data down to TCP A for transmission with a function call. We assume 50 octets are to be sent. TCP A encapsulates this data into a segment, sends the segment to TCP B with sequence number = 101, as depicted in event 2. Remember that this sequence number is used to number the first octet of the user data stream.

At the remote TCP, data is delivered to the user (ULP B) in event 3, and TCP B acknowledges the data with a segment acknowledgment number = 151. This is depicted in event 4. The acknowledgment number of 151 acknowledges inclusively the 50 octets transmitted in the segment depicted in event 2.

Next, the user connected to TCP B sends data in event 5. This data is encapsulated into a segment and transmitted as event 6 in the dia-

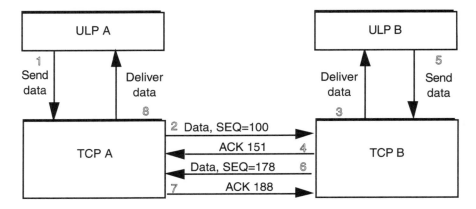

Figure B–14   TCP data transfer operations

gram. This initial sequence number from TCP B was 177. Therefore, TCP begins its sequencing with 178. In this example, it transmits 10 octets.

TCP A acknowledges TCP B's 10 segments in event 7 by returning a segment with acknowledgment number = 188. In event 8, this data is delivered to TCP A's user.

Figure B–15 shows a close operation. Event 1 illustrates that TCP A's user wishes to close its operations with its upper peer layer protocol at TCP B. The effect of close is shown in event 2, where TCP A sends a segment with the FIN bit set to 1. The sequence number of 151 is a continuation of the operation shown in the previous figure. This is the next sequence number the TCP module is required to send.

The effect of this transmitted segment is shown as event 3 from TCP B, which acknowledges TCP A's FIN SEQ 151. Its segment contains ACK = 152. Next, it issues a closing call to its user, which is depicted as event 4.

In this example, the user application acknowledges and grants the close in event 5. It may or may not execute the close depending on the state of its operations. However, for simplicity, we assume the event depicted in 5 does occur. The information in this function is mapped to event 6, which is the final segment issued by TCP B. Notice that in event 6, the FIN flag is set to 1, and SEQ = 188. Finally, TCP A acknowledges this final segment with event 7 as ACK = 189.

The result of all these operations is shown in events 8 and 9, where connection closed signals are sent to the user applications.

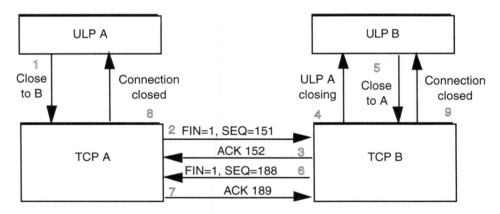

Figure B–15   TCP close operations

HOW TRAFFIC IS TRANSPORTED ACROSS THE INTERNET

Figure B–16 shows a typical internet layered architecture for both a public and private network. This analysis is presented in a general way here, and in more detail later.

At the bottom part of the figure, we find router A and three hosts attached to an Ethernet. Two of the hosts are running the IP protocol family (hosts A and C) and host B is running IBM's Systems Network Architecture (SNA) protocol suite. The notation ULPs connotes that the hosts are running IP-specific or SNA-specific upper layer protocols. At host B, IBM's layer 3 is the Path Control Protocol (labeled in this figure IBM Path). Router A is running multiple protocol families. While this example shows only two protocol families (IP and SNA), routers typically support several other protocol families such as DECnet, AppleTalk, X.25, etc.

Notice that all four machines (router A, and hosts A, B, and C) are running Ethernet's layer 1 (L_1) layer 2 (L_2: media access control [MAC]). At router A, the outbound links to routers B and C are configured with T1 at the physical layer. At the data link layer (L_2), the point-to-point protocol (PPP) is used for the IP link and IBM's Synchronous Data Link Control (SDLC) is used on the SNA link.

When the traffic is passed to either router B or router C, these routers examine the destination address in the layer 3 header to make forwarding decisions. This operation is depicted in router B with the IP module [at an Internet Service Provider (ISP)] and in router C with the IBM Path module. When the layer-3 protocols make their forwarding decisions, the layer-3 header and the upper-layer traffic is passed to the outgoing links L_2 protocol which (once again) is PPP in the internet-based router and SDLC in the SNA-based router.

Next, the traffic is placed in a layer 1 (L_1) protocol data unit to be sent across either the public Internet or the private SNA network. As the figure shows, the internet traffic is transported by SONET at layer 1 and the SNA traffic is transported by the T3 carrier system. There is no restriction on the choice of the physical layers; they are used here to illustrate two options.

At routers D and E and subsequently at routers F and hosts D, E, and F, the processes just described are reversed, with the traffic placed on the receiving Ethernet and sent to the specific host on this network at the top of the figure.

Thus, the complete transmissions in these examples traverse through different types of networks as well as different transmission media. This example is sufficient to demonstrate the relationships of

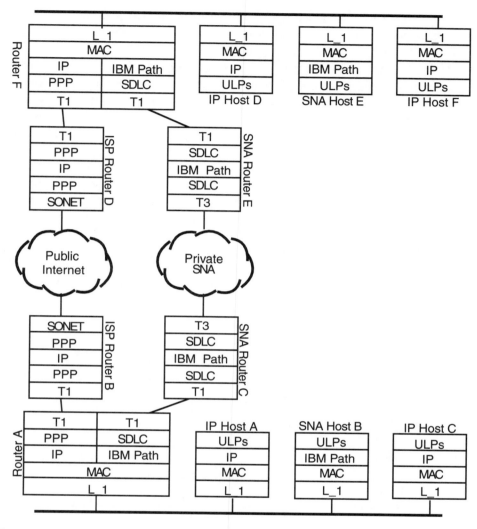

Where:
  IP   Internet Protocol (layer 3 of the Internet protocol suite)
  MAC   Media access control (layer 2 of Ethernet)
  PPP   Point-to-Point Protocol (layer 2 of many IP interfaces)
  SDLC   Synchronous Data Link Control (layer 2 of SNA)
  ULPs   Upper layer protocols (typically layers 4 through 7)
  SNA   Systems Network Architecture (IBM's data communications system)
  ISP   Internet service provider

Figure B–16   Typical topology for an Internet

local and wide area networks and their corresponding layers. The next discussions will focus in more detail on how these operations come about.

To continue this analysis, Figure B–17 shows the format of the Ethernet frame that is transmitted across the Ethernet link. We stated that two different protocol "families" are supported on this Ethernet LAN, the Internet Protocol (IP) and the Systems Network Architecture (SNA). The addresses in the Ethernet frame are conventional MAC addresses. The Ethertype field in Ethernet is used to identify the different protocol families that are running on the network.

The preamble is transmitted first to achieve medium stabilization and synchronization. The destination address can identify an individual workstation on the network or a group of stations. A cyclic redundancy check (CRC) value is contained in the frame check sequence (FCS) field for error detection operations.

The IEEE specifies values to identify Ethertype assignments. Some of the codes are contained in Table B–1. Their purpose is to identify the upper-layer protocol (ULP) that is running on the LAN, typically at L_3.

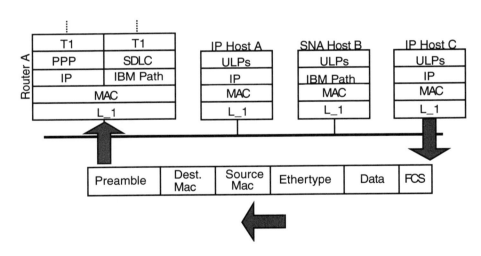

Where:
FCS   Frame check sequence
IP   Internet Protocol
MAC   Media access control
PPP   Point-to-Point Protocol
SDLC   Synchronous Data Link Control
ULPs   Upper layer protocols

Figure B–17   An Internet LAN

Table B–1   Ethertype assignments (examples)

Ethernet Decimal	Hex	Description
2048	0800	DoD Internet Protocol (IP)
2049	0801	X.75 Internet
2051	0803	ECMA Internet
2053	0805	X.25 level 3
2054	0806	Address Resolution Protocol (ARP)
2055	0807	XNS compatibility
4096	1000	Berkeley Trailer
21000	5208	BBN Simnet
24579	6003	DEC DECnet Phase IV
24580	6004	DEC LAT
32773	8005	HP Probe
32821	8035	Reverse ARP
32824	8038	DEC LANBridge
32823	8098	AppleTalk

After the local router processes the IP datagram and makes routing decisions regarding the next node that is to receive the datagram, this datagram is passed to this next node (see Figure B–18).

It is possible that the next node is on the same network as the sending host. In this situation, the router relays the datagram back onto the LAN from which the datagram originated. For this example, the figure highlights the routers involved in transporting the datagram through a wide area network (or networks) to the final destination.

Notice that routers B, C, D, and E are not configured with the LAN interfaces. They perform the function of wide area network relay systems. In most installations, these routers have LAN interfaces but they are not germane to this discussion.

Figure B–19 depicts the operations on the outgoing link of the router which received the Ethernet frame across a local interface. Notice that the protocol data unit on the left side of the figure differs from the protocol data unit originally sent to the router. This protocol data unit is an example of a Point-to-Point Protocol (PPP) frame.

The specific contents of each field in the PPP frame are beyond this discussion. The relevant aspects of the frame contents are the protocol ID

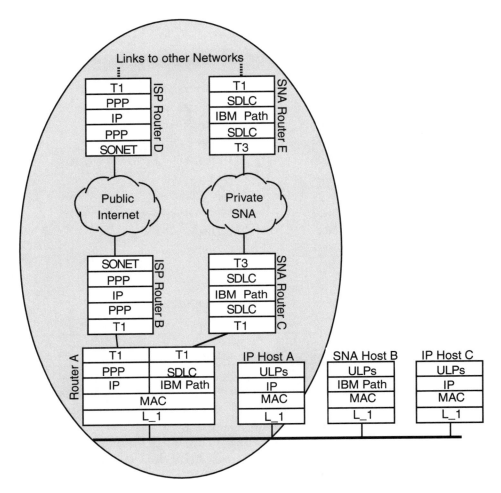

Figure B–18   An Internet WAN

field and the data field. The protocol ID field provides the same function as the Ethernet Ethertype field. It identifies the type of traffic residing in the data field. The router's task is to map the Ethertype value to the PPP protocol ID field, since the LAN L_2 Ethernet headers and trailers are stripped away and replaced with the WAN L_2 PPP headers and trailers.

Figure B–20 shows that the traffic is now passed to a T1 link. At this stage of the operation, the PPP frame is placed into a T1 DS0 channel (or channels). The traffic is shipped across the T1 link to a network service provider, and in this example, the ISP's router B.

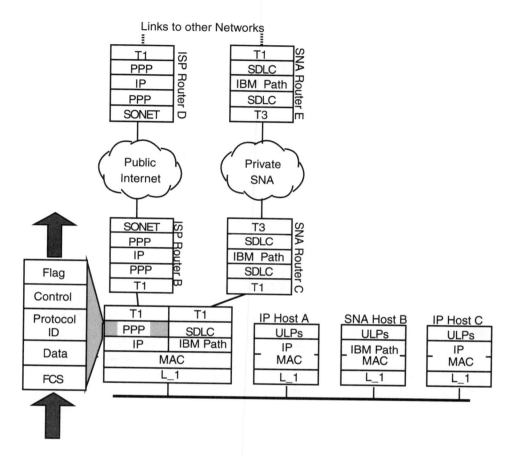

Figure B–19   Presenting the traffic to the WAN

The manner in which T1 supports data communications varies and the reader should check the specific vendor implementations. In some systems, the data traffic is not slotted into discrete DS0 channels. In others, it is placed precisely into the DS0 slots on a periodic basis.

We now find the datagram being processed by router B in Figure B–21. Notice that the PPP headers and trailers have been stripped away and the router examines the IP datagram header which resides in the data field of the arriving protocol data unit.

The router compares the destination IP address in this datagram to IP addresses stored in a routing table. Following various rules on IP address searching operations (discussed later), a match will reveal the next node that is to receive the datagram. If a match occurs successfully, the

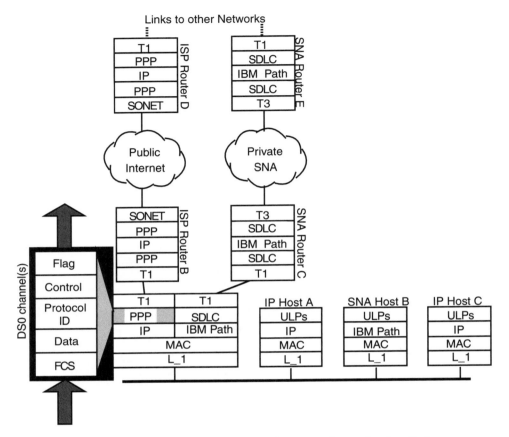

Figure B–20   Relaying the traffic onto the outgoing link

router (in this example) places the data field inside a layer-2 frame (PPP in this case) and sends the frame to the outgoing physical layer, which in this example is a SONET (Synchronous Optical Network) link. In effect, the traffic is encapsulated into a SONET frame.

In many of the high-capacity links in the Internet, SONET has replaced the T1/T3 trunks, as shown in Figure B–22. The SONET OC-3 rate (optical carrier) of 155 Mbit/s is more attractive than the slower 1.5 Mbit/s T1 and 45 Mbit/s T3 trunks. In addition, SONET has other significant advantages over the T1 technology.

First, SONET is built on fiber optic standards which provide for superior performance vis-à-vis the copper-cable systems. SONET also provides the ability to combine and consolidate traffic from different loca-

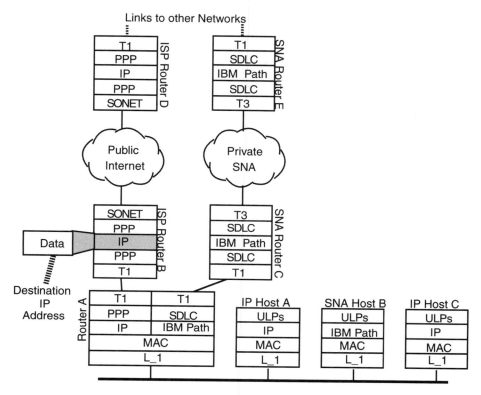

Figure B–21   At an intermediate router

tions through one facility. This concept, known as grooming, eliminates inefficient techniques that are part of the T1 operation.

SONET has notably improved network management features relative to current technology, and uses extensive headers to provide information on diagnostics, configurations, and alarms. In addition, SONET can be configured with a number of topologies, some of which can provide for robustness in the form of backup links, and the ability to divert traffic around problem nodes or links.

The datagram continues its journey through the Internet, through the terminating IP node (router D in Figure B–23) and to the local router that services the destination host's network (router F in this example). The process depicted by the arrows in this figure, is identical to the operations that occurred at the originating nodes except in reverse order. Therefore, we shall not revisit them here.

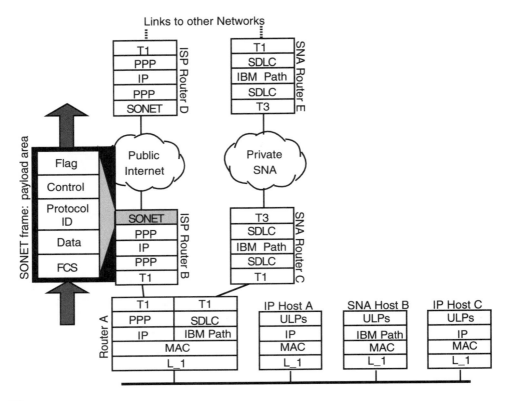

Where:
SONET   Synchronous Optical Network

Figure B–22   Using SONET

In Figure B–24, after the datagram has arrived at router F (which has demultiplexed the IP traffic from the T1 frame, and has processed the PPP frame as well), it examines the destination IP address in the IP datagram header to determine the recipient of this datagram. Once this determination has been made, router F: (a) resolves the destination IP address to the destination MAC address, (b) encapsulates the data field into an Ethernet MAC frame and (c) maps the PPP protocol ID field into the Ethernet Ethertype field. The traffic is then sent out onto the local network in the Ethernet frame.

To conclude this overview, in Figure B–25 we now see the Ethernet frame being send from router F to IP host F. Inside the data field resides

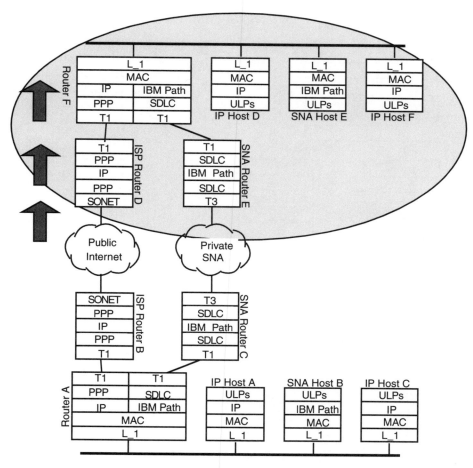

Figure B–23   Delivery to the receiving network

the IP datagram which (among other values) contains the IP source address and IP destination address. The MAC addresses identify the source MAC address which is router F and the destination MAC address which is host F.

This completes our analyses of the traffic flow between local and wide area networks. It is a general view and further analyses will provide more details on these operations.

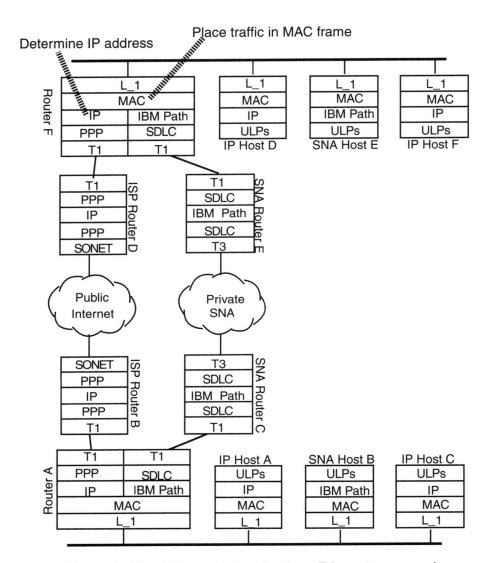

Figure B–24   Address determination, Ethernet encapsulation

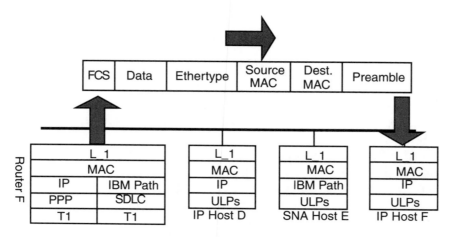

Figure B–25   The final transmission

THE DOMAIN NAME SYSTEM (DNS)

This section examines the Domain Name System (DNS) specification and its UNIX-based implementation, the Berkeley Internet Name Domain (BIND) system. These systems provide name server operations. This means that their principal function is to map (or correlate) a "user-friendly" e-mail name to a routeable address.

This type of service is quite helpful to a user, because the user is not tasked with remembering an abstract address of a person (or application) with whom the user wishes to communicate. Rather, the sending user need only know a "easy-to-remember" text-oriented value (a name) of the recipient. This name is keyed-in during a session, relayed to a name server, which looks up an associated address.

So, DNS and BIND are similar to ARP. They correlate (map) one identifier to another. But the correlations are different. ARP maps layer 2 addresses to/from layer 3 address, or layer 2/3 addresses to/from virtual circuit identifiers. Whereas, DNS/BIND correlate names to/from addresses.

The Internet Protocol (IP) address structure (consisting of 32 bits) is somewhat awkward to use by humans. Indeed, instead of using the IP address, many users have adapted the use of acronyms, and meaningful terms to identify a numeric address. This practice presents an interesting problem if a network user is using acronyms, etc. as an address and must internetwork with a network that uses the numeric IP addresses. How is the non-IP identifier mapped to an IP address?

One could say that the user should conform and learn to use the IP addresses. Yet, we cannot expect an end user to remember all the values on these addresses, much less to key in these addresses at the workstation. The solution is to devise a naming scheme wherein an end user can employ a friendly, easy-to-remember name to identify the sending and receiving entities.

In order for this idea to be implemented, procedures must first be established to provide (a) a framework for establishing user friendly names and (b) conventions for mapping the names to IP addresses.

In the Internet, the organization and managing of these names was provided originally by the SRI Network Information Center. It maintained a file called HOST.TXT which listed the names of networks, gateways, and hosts and their corresponding addresses.

The original structure of *flat-name* spaces worked well enough in the early days of internet. This term describes a form of a name consisting merely of characters identifying an object without any further meaning or structure. As stated earlier, the Internet Network Information

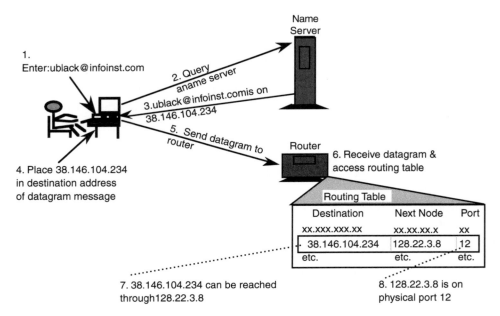

Figure B–26   Operations with name servers

Center was responsible for administering name spaces and assigning them to new objects that were identified in internet.

Figure B–26 shows the approach used today. In event 1, a person enters a domain name for Uyless Black: ublack@infoinst.com. The name server software in the host forms a query to a local name server (event 2). In effect, this query asks the name server to look up the name in the DNA database and find an associated address. In event 3, the name server responds with a reply which associates ublack@infoinst.com to address 38.146.104.234.

In event 4, this address is placed into the destination IP address field of the IP datagram and in event 5, it is sent to a local router. The router receives the datagram (event 6), and finds a match in its routing table with the identification address in the datagram (event 7), which reveals the node to receive the datagram, as well as the outgoing physical port (interface) through which the datagram is transported to the next node (event 8).

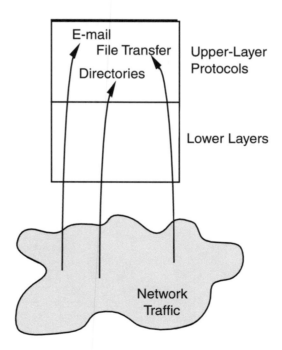

Figure B–27   Upper-layer identifiers

UPPER LAYER IDENTIFIERS

Physical and network level addresses are insufficient to move the packet to its final "destination" on the host machine, and other higher layer identifiers are needed. For example, a packet may be destined for a specific software application, such as an email or a file transfer system. Since both these applications reside in the same upper layer (the application layer), some means must be devised to identify the application that is to process the packet. An identifier is used by the host machine to determine which application receives the data.

The upper layer names are identified by a variety of terms. The Internet convention is to use the terms port and socket. The OSI convention is to use the term service access point (SAP), see Figure B–27.

Abbreviations

A Application Layer
ABM Asynchronous Balanced Mode
ACCM Async Control Character Map
ACK Positively Acknowledged
ACKs TCP acknowledgments
AHDL Asynchronous HDLC
API Application Programming Interface
APPN-HPR Advanced Peer-to-Peer Networking High-Performance Routing
ARP Address Resolution Protocol
ATM Asynchronous Transfer Mode
AVP Attribute-Value-Pair
BAP Bandwidth Allocation Protocol
BACP Bandwidth Allocation Control Protocol
BIND Berkeley Internet Name Domain
BOD Bandwidth-on-Demand
BRI basic rate interface
C bit cost bit
CCP Compression Control Protocol
CDMA Code Division Multiple Access
CDPD Cellular Digital Packet Data

CDN called party number
CHAP Challenge-Handshake Authentication Protocol
CLNP Connectionless-Layer Network Protocol
CND Call Disconnect Notify
CPI Common Part Indicator
CRC Cyclic Redundancy Check
CTA Concatenated Tunnel Approach
CTS Clear to Send
cwnd Congestion Window
D Data Link Layer
DA Destination IP Address
D bit delay bit
DCE Data Circuit Terminating Equipment
DF Don't Fragment
DISC Disconnect
DLC Data Link Control
DM Disconnect Mode
DNS Domain Name System
DP Destination Port Number
DSU data service unit
DTE Data Terminal Equipment
ECP Encryption Control Protocol

EOT   End of Transmission

ESF   Extended Super Frame

ESP   Enhanced Service Provider

F   Flags

FCS   frame check sequence

FDDI   Fiber distributed data interface

FIN   finish message

FTP   File Transfer Protocol

FUNI   Frame User Network Interface

GSM   Global Systems for Mobile Communications

HDLC   High-Level Data Link Control

I   Information

IANA   Internet Assigned Numbers Authority

ICCN   Incoming Call Connected

ICMP   Internet Control Message Protocol

ICRP   Incoming Call Reply

ICRQ   Incoming Call Request

IGMP   Internet Group Message Protocol

IP   Internet Protocol

IPCP   IP Control Protocol

IPSec   Internet Security Protocol

IPX   Internet Packet Exchange

IPXCP   Internet Packet Exchange Network Control Protocol

ISDN   Integrated Services Digital Network

ISO   International Standards Organization

ISP   Internet Service Provider

ISS   Initial Send Sequence

ITA   Independent Tunnel Approach

IWF   interworking function

LAC   L2TP Access Concentrator

LAN   Local Area Network

LAPB   Link Access Procedure, Balanced

LAPD   Link Access Procedure for the D Channel

LAPDm   LAPD for Mobile Links

LAPF   LAP for Frame Relay

LAPM   Link Access Procedure for Modems

LAPX   Link Access Procedure, Half-Duplex

LCP   Link Control Protocol

LDQR   Link Drop Query Request

LEC   Local Exchange Carrier

LLC   Logical Link Control

LNS   L2TP Network Server

LQS   Link Quality Monitoring

L2TP   Layer 2 Tunneling Protocol

MAC   Media Access Control

MDLP   Mobile Data Link Protocol

MLP   Multilink Procedures

MP   Multilink Protocol

MRRU   Multilink Maximum Received Reconstructed Unit

MSS   Maximum Segment Size

MTP   Message Transfer Port

MTU   Maximum Transmission Unit

N   Network Layer

NAK   Negatively Acknowledged

NAS   Network Access Server

NAT   Network Address Translation

NBNS   NET-BIOS Name Server

NCP   Network Control Protocol

NLPID   Network Level Protocol Identification

NRZI   Non Return to Zero Inverted

OCCN   Outgoing Call Connected

OCRP   Outgoing Call Replay

OCRQ   Outgoing Call Request

OSI   Open Systems Interconnection

OSPF   Open Shortest Path First

OUI   Organizational Unique Identifier

P   padding

P   Physical Layer

PAD   Padding bytes

PAP   Password Authentication Protocol

PC   Personal Computer

PCI   Protocol Control Information

PDU   protocol data unit

PFC   Protocol Field Compression
PID   Protocol Identification
PPP   Point-to-Point Protocol
PRI   primary rate interface
PSH   Push Message
PSTN   Public Switched Telephone Network
PVC   Permanent Virtual Circuit
QOS   Quality-of-Service
RADIUS   Remote Authentication Dial-In User Service
RARP   Reverse Address Resolution Protocol
R bit   Reliability bit
RD   Request Disconnect
REJ   Reject
RES   Reset
RFC   Request for Comments
RIM   Request Initialization Mode
RIP   Routing Information Protocol
RNR   Receive Not Ready
RPC   remote procedure call
RR   Receive Ready
RST   reset message
RTS   Request to Send
SA   Source IP Address
SAA   Simple AVP Approach
SABM   Set Asynchronous Balanced Mode
SABME   Set Asynchronous Balanced Mode Extended
SAP   Service Access Point
SARM   Set Asynchronous Response Mode
SCCCN   Start Control Connection Connected
SCCRP   Start Control Connection Reply
SCCRQ   Start Control Connection Request
SDLC   Synchronous Data Link Control
SEQ   Sequence
SLI   Set Link Info

SLIP   Serial Link IP
SMTP   Simple Mail Transfer Protocol
SNA   Systems Network Architecture
SNACP   Systems Network Architecture Network Control Protocol
SNAP   Subnetwork Access Protocol
SNMP   Simple Network Management Protocol
SNRM   Set Normal Response Mode
SNRME   Set Normal Response Mode Extended
SONET   Synchronous Optical Network
SP   Source Port Number
SPE   Synchronous Payload Envelope
SPI   Security Parameter Index
SREJ   Selective Reject
SS7   Signaling System Number 7
Stop CCN   Stop Control Connection Notification
SVC   Switched Virtual Call
SYN   Synchronize Message
T   Transport Layer
TA   terminal adapter
T bit   throughput bit
TCP   Transmission Control Protocol
TEST   Test
TFTP   Trivial File Transfer Protocol
TOS   Type of Service
TTL   time-to-live
UA   unnumbered acknowledgment
UI   Unnumbered information
UDP   user datagram protocol
ULP   Upper Layer Protocol
UNI   User Network Interface
UP   Unnumbered Poll
URG   Urgent Message
VPDN   Virtual Private Dial Network
V(R)   Receive State Variable
V(S)   Send State Variable
WAN   Wide Area Network
WEN   WAN Error Notification
XID   exchange ID

Index